Emotionally Healthy Spirituality

WORKBOOK

The Emotionally Healthy Discipleship Course

by Peter and Geri Scazzero

A proven strategy that moves people from shallow discipleship to deep transformation in Christ.

PART 1

Introducing people to a transformative spirituality with God.

Emotionally Healthy Spirituality

- Eight-session DVD video study
- Workbook plus Streaming Video access
- Book
- Day by Day devotional

PART 2

Practical skills to launch people into a transformative spirituality with others.

Emotionally Healthy Relationships

- Eight-session DVD video study
- Workbook plus Streaming Video access
- Day by Day devotional

ALSO BY PETER SCAZZERO

The Emotionally Healthy Leader
The Emotionally Healthy Woman (with Geri Scazzero)
Emotionally Healthy Discipleship

Emotionally Healthy Spirituality

DISCIPLESHIP THAT DEEPLY CHANGES
YOUR RELATIONSHIP WITH GOD

EXPANDED EDITION

WORKBOOK
EIGHT SESSIONS

Peter and Geri Scazzero

Emotionally Healthy Spirituality Workbook, Expanded Edition

Requests for information should be addressed to:
HarperChristian Resources, *3900 Sparks Dr. SE, Grand Rapids, Michigan 49546*

ISBN 978-0-310-13173-1 (softcover)
ISBN 978-0-310-13174-8 (ebook)

HarperChristian Resources titles may be purchased in bulk for churches, business, fundraising, or ministry use. For information, please e-mail ResourceSpecialist@ChurchSource.com.

Cover photography: Shutterstock
Author photos: Orlando Suazo
Interior design: Beth Shagene
Interior iceberg illustration: 123RF® / Ion Popa

First Printing November 2021 / Printed in the United States of America

25 26 27 28 29 LBC 15 14 13 12 11

Contents

Introduction vii
How to Use This Workbook ix
Guidelines for the Group. xi

SESSION 1
The Problem of Emotionally Unhealthy Spirituality 1

SESSION 2
Know Yourself That You May Know God 15

SESSION 3
Going Back in Order to Go Forward. 27

SESSION 4
Journey through the Wall 39

SESSION 5
Enlarge Your Soul through Grief and Loss 51

SESSION 6
Discover the Rhythms of the Daily Office and Sabbath 61

SESSION 7
Grow into an Emotionally Mature Adult 77

SESSION 8
Go the Next Step to Develop a "Rule of Life" 91

Leader's Guide. 103
Notes 121
About the Authors 123
Checklist for the Emotionally Healthy (EH) Spirituality Course. 132

Introduction

Emotionally Healthy Spirituality, which is Part 1 of the *Emotionally Healthy Discipleship Course*, is a plan for discipleship that deeply changes our relationship with God.

EH Spirituality does this in two ways:

1. Addressing directly the reality that emotional maturity and spiritual maturity are inseparable, that it is not possible to be spiritually mature while remaining emotionally immature.
2. Equipping people in a personal, firsthand relationship with Jesus by incorporating stillness, silence, and Scripture as daily life rhythms.

The goal of this workbook, along with its companion resources—*the EH Spirituality Course* video, the *Emotionally Healthy Spirituality* book, and the *Emotionally Healthy Spirituality Day by Day* devotional—is to help you implement the eight core biblical truths that make up *EH Spirituality.* On the last page of the workbook, you will find a checklist. Fill it out along the way and, when completed, go to emotionallyhealthy.org to receive your certificate of completion. We also strongly encourage you to go to www.emotionallyhealthy.org/vault to access a number of other free resources.

Each of the eight truths explored in these sessions could easily have been expanded into their own course. We have kept them together, however, to serve as an introduction into a life with God that goes beyond "tip of the iceberg spirituality" into transformation through Christ that touches the depth of your being.

How to Use This Workbook

Before Session 1

- Purchase the *Emotionally Healthy Spirituality* book, *Emotionally Healthy Spirituality Day by Day*, and this workbook.
- Read chapter 1 of the *Emotionally Healthy Spirituality* book.
- A seven-minute video that introduces how to use *Emotionally Healthy Spirituality Day by Day* can be found at www.emotionallyhealthy.org/vault or on YouTube.

Throughout the Study

The key to receive the impact of this workbook is what comes around it. Each week you will be asked to read a chapter of the book from the *Emotionally Healthy Spirituality* book before the session, engage the workbook during the session, and read the corresponding *EH Spirituality Day by Day* devotionals after the session. The chart on the next page gives you a visual roadmap for what to do each week.

You will also find at the end of each session in this workbook a "Between-Sessions Personal Study" section. This is based on questions from the Daily Offices found in the *Emotionally Healthy Spirituality Day by Day* devotional.

The Leader's Guide in the back of this workbook provides extremely helpful information to supplement the studies. We encourage you to avail yourselves of this valuable material. Additional free resources for this course can be found at www.emotionallyhealthy.org/vault.

	 BEFORE the session		 AFTER the session
	Read Emotionally Healthy Spirituality Book	**DURING** the session use the EHS Workbook	Read EHS Day by Day Optional: Fill out Reflection Questions
SESSION 1 The Problem of Emotionally Unhealthy Spirituality	Introduction & Chapter 1	Engage in Workbook activities with videos	Week 1
SESSION 2 Know Yourself that You May Know God	Chapter 2	Engage in Workbook activities with videos	Week 2
SESSION 3 Go Back to Go Forward	Chapter 3	Engage in Workbook activities with videos	Week 3
SESSION 4 Journey Through the Wall	Chapter 4	Engage in Workbook activities with videos	Week 4
SESSION 5 Enlarge Your Heart Through Grief and Loss	Chapter 5	Engage in Workbook activities with videos	Week 5
SESSION 6 Discover the Rhythms of the Daily Office and Sabbath	Chapter 6	Engage in Workbook activities with videos	Week 6
SESSION 7 Grow into an Emotionally Mature Adult	Chapter 7	Engage in Workbook activities with videos	Week 7
SESSION 8 Develop a Rule of Life	Chapter 8	Engage in Workbook activities with videos	Week 8

Important Note on the Videos

The *Introduction* and *Closing Summary* video presentations for each session are available FREE through streaming access for you to review each week. Simply use the code found on the inside front cover of the workbook.

You can also access them wherever books/DVDs are sold, or by digital video through sites such as amazon.com, vimeo.com, and christianbook.com.

Guidelines for the Group

Be Prepared

To get the most out of your time together, we ask that you read the chapters in *Emotionally Healthy Spirituality* that correspond with each session. Please also bring your workbook and the *EH Spirituality Day by Day* book with you to each meeting.

Speak for Yourself

We encourage you to share and use "I" statements. We are only experts on ourselves. For example: Instead of saying, "Everyone is busy," say, "I am busy." Instead of saying, "We all struggle with forgiving," say, "I struggle with forgiving."

Respect Others

Be brief in your sharing, remaining mindful that there are time limitations and others may want to share.

No Fixing, Saving, No Setting Other People Straight

Respect people's journeys and trust the Holy Spirit inside of them to lead them into all truth—in his timing. Resist the temptation to offer quick advice as people share in the group.

Turn to Wonder

If you feel judgmental or defensive when someone else is sharing, ask yourself: *I wonder what brought him/her to this belief? I wonder what he/she is feeling right now? I wonder what my reaction teaches me about myself?*

Trust and Learn from Silence

It is okay to have silence between responses as the group shares, giving members the opportunity to reflect. Remember, there is no pressure to share.

Observe Confidentiality

In order to create an environment that is safe for open and honest participation, anything someone shares within the group should not be repeated outside of the group. However, feel free to share your own story and personal growth.

Punctuality

Resolve to arrive on time.

SESSION 1

The Problem of Emotionally Unhealthy Spirituality

Before your first group meeting, read chapter 1 of the *Emotionally Healthy Spirituality* book.

Daily Office (10 minutes)

Do one of the Daily Offices from Week 1 of *Emotionally Healthy Spirituality Day by Day* to begin your session. **(Leaders, please see point number two in the "General Guidelines" on page 105.)**

Introduction (3 minutes)

Emotional health and spiritual maturity cannot be separated. It is not possible to be spiritually mature while remaining emotionally immature.

When we ignore the emotional component of our lives, we move through the motions of Christian disciplines, activities, and behaviors, but deeply rooted behavioral patterns from our pasts continue to hinder us from an authentic life of maturity in Christ.

We often neglect to reflect on what is going on inside us and around us (emotional health) and are too busy to slow down to be with God (contemplative spirituality).[1] As a result, we run the high risk of remaining stuck as spiritual infants, failing to develop into spiritually/emotionally mature adults in Christ.

Jay, one of our church members, described it best: "I was a Christian for twenty-two years. But instead of being a twenty-two-year-old Christian, I was a one-year-old Christian twenty-two times! I just kept doing the same things over and over and over again."

In order to facilitate a sense of safety at each small group table, please turn to pages xi–xii as the "Guidelines for the Group" are read aloud.

Growing Connected (10 minutes)

Share your name and a few words about what makes you feel fully alive (e.g., nature, music, sports, reading, cooking).

VIDEO: The Problem of Emotionally Unhealthy Spirituality (11 minutes)

Watch the video teaching segment for Session 1 and use the space provided to note anything that stands out to you.

NOTES

Group Discussion (45 minutes)

Starters (10 minutes)

The following are the top ten symptoms of emotionally *unhealthy* spirituality. As the list that begins below is read aloud, put a check mark next to the one or two symptoms that are most relevant in your life today.

☐ **1. Using God to run from God**

(*Example:* I keep myself busy in church activities to avoid the pain and tension I'm experiencing in my close relationships.)

☐ **2. Ignoring the emotions of anger, sadness, and fear**

(*Example:* I am rarely honest with myself and/or others about the feelings, hurts, and pains beneath the surface of my life.)

- ☐ **3. Dying to the wrong things**
  (*Example:* I tend to deny healthy, God-given desires and pleasures of life such as friendships, joy, music, beauty, laughter, and nature. At the same time, I find it difficult to die to my self-protectiveness, defensiveness, lack of vulnerability, and judgmentalism.)
- ☐ **4. Denying the past's impact on the present**
  (*Example:* I rarely consider how my family of origin and significant people/events from my past have shaped my present.)
- ☐ **5. Dividing life into "secular" and "sacred" compartments**
  (*Example:* I easily compartmentalize God to "Christian activities" while usually forgetting about him when I am working, shopping, studying, or recreating.)
- ☐ **6. Doing for God instead of being with God**
  (*Example:* I tend to evaluate my spirituality based on how much I am doing for God.)
- ☐ **7. Spiritualizing away conflict**
  (*Example:* I usually miss out on true peace by smoothing over disagreements, burying tensions, and avoiding conflict, rather than disrupting false peace as Jesus did.)
- ☐ **8. Covering over brokenness, weakness, and failure**
  (*Example:* I have a hard time speaking freely about my weaknesses, failures, and mistakes.)
- ☐ **9. Living without limits**
  (*Example:* Those close to me would say that I often "try to do it all" or "bite off more than I can chew.")
- ☐ **10. Judging the spiritual journeys of others**
  (*Example*: I often find myself occupied and bothered by the faults of those around me.)

Afterward, turn to another person and each share the one symptom that most applies to your spiritual life today.

Bible Study: 1 Samuel 15:7–24 (35 minutes)

In this story we meet King Saul, the first king of Israel, and Samuel, God's prophet who brings God's word to Saul. King Saul had been instructed by God earlier in verse 3 to "attack the Amalekites and totally destroy all that belongs to them." (Note: The Amalekites were a wicked, sinful culture known for their destructiveness).

Saul, however, gives in to the wishes of his fighting men and does *only part* of God's will. Read aloud 1 Samuel 15:7–24.

> 7 Then Saul attacked the Amalekites all the way from Havilah to Shur, near the eastern border of Egypt. 8 He took Agag king of the Amalekites alive, and all his people he totally destroyed with the sword. 9 But Saul and the army spared Agag and the best of the sheep and cattle, the fat calves and lambs—everything that was good. These they were unwilling to destroy completely, but everything that was despised and weak they totally destroyed.
>
> 10 Then the word of the LORD came to Samuel: 11 "I regret that I have made Saul king, because he has turned away from me and has not carried out my instructions." Samuel was angry, and he cried out to the LORD all that night.
>
> 12 Early in the morning Samuel got up and went to meet Saul, but he was told, "Saul has gone to Carmel. There he has set up a monument in his own honor and has turned and gone on down to Gilgal."
>
> 13 When Samuel reached him, Saul said, "The LORD bless you! I have carried out the LORD's instructions."
>
> 14 But Samuel said, "What then is this bleating of sheep in my ears? What is this lowing of cattle that I hear?"
>
> 15 Saul answered, "The soldiers brought them from the Amalekites; they spared the best of the sheep and cattle to sacrifice to the LORD your God, but we totally destroyed the rest."
>
> 16 "Enough!" Samuel said to Saul. "Let me tell you what the LORD said to me last night."
>
> "Tell me," Saul replied.
>
> 17 Samuel said, "Although you were once small in your own eyes, did you not become the head of the tribes of Israel? The LORD anointed you king over Israel. 18 And he sent you on a mission, saying, 'Go and completely destroy those wicked people, the Amalekites; wage war against them until you have wiped them out.' 19 Why did you not obey the LORD? Why did you pounce on the plunder and do evil in the eyes of the LORD?"
>
> 20 "But I did obey the LORD," Saul said. "I went on the mission the LORD assigned me. I completely destroyed the Amalekites and brought back Agag their king. 21 The

soldiers took sheep and cattle from the plunder, the best of what was devoted to God, in order to sacrifice them to the LORD your God at Gilgal."

22 But Samuel replied:

"Does the LORD delight in burnt offerings and sacrifices
as much as in obeying the LORD?
To obey is better than sacrifice,
and to [listen] is better than the fat of rams.
23 For rebellion is like the sin of divination,
and arrogance like the evil of idolatry.
Because you have rejected the word of the LORD,
he has rejected you as king."

24 Then Saul said to Samuel, "I have sinned. I violated the LORD's command and your instructions. I was afraid of the men and so I gave in to them."

1. In verses 10 and 11, what words and phrases reveal the depth of God's and Samuel's feelings around the choices Saul made? Contrast that with Saul's response in verses 12 and 13? (4 minutes)

2. Rereading verses 12, 15, and 24, how would you describe the things Saul was unaware of within himself? (6 minutes)

3. Saul's unawareness leads him to go through the motions of religious activity as enough. The offering of sacrifices at that time would be equal to our religious activity today. Saul makes sacrifices, but he doesn't obey or listen to God (see v. 22). What might be one example of how you do religious activity, but it is disconnected from your heart and life? (e.g., I go to church but can't stand people at work who irritate or hurt me; I serve in church but spend little time developing my own relationship with Jesus; I say I follow Jesus but rarely pray or consult with him before making decisions) (7 minutes)

4. Saul pretends to be someone on the outside that he is not on the inside, (i.e., a false self). Use the following symptoms of a false self to get an idea of where you are right now. Next to each statement write down the number that best describes your response. Use the following scale:

5 = Always true of me
4 = Frequently true of me
3 = Occasionally true of me
2 = Rarely true of me
1 = Never true of me

1. I compare myself a lot to other people. ___
2. I often say "yes" when I prefer to say "no." ___
3. I often don't speak up to avoid the disapproval of others. ___
4. People close to me would describe me as defensive and easily offended. ___
5. I have a hard time laughing at my shortcomings and failures. ___
6. I avoid looking weak or foolish in social situations. ___
7. I am not always the person I appear to be. ___
8. I struggle with taking risks because I could fail or look foolish. ___

9. My sense of worth/well-being comes from what I have (possessions), what I do (accomplishments), or what others think of me (popularity). ___
10. I often act like a different person when in different situations and with different people. ___

Share the one that most stands out to you with your table (or in groups of two or three). (11 minutes)

5. What might be one invitation from God for you out of this entire story about Saul? (12 minutes)

Application (15 minutes)

After the following paragraphs and questions 1 and 2 are read aloud, take 5 minutes to journal your response to those questions in the space provided. Then share your response to question 3 in groups of two or three.

Not only was Saul unaware of what was going on inside of him, he also did not cultivate a contemplative life with God. His "doing" for God did not flow from his "being" with God.

In the same way, our "doing" for Jesus must flow from our "being" with him. Far too often, we live vicariously off other people's spirituality and relate to God while busily "on the run."

1. What challenges keep you from slowing down your life to be with God?

2. The diagram below provides an illustration of a spiritual life where our activity (i.e., our doing) is out of balance with our contemplative life (i.e., our inner life with Jesus).

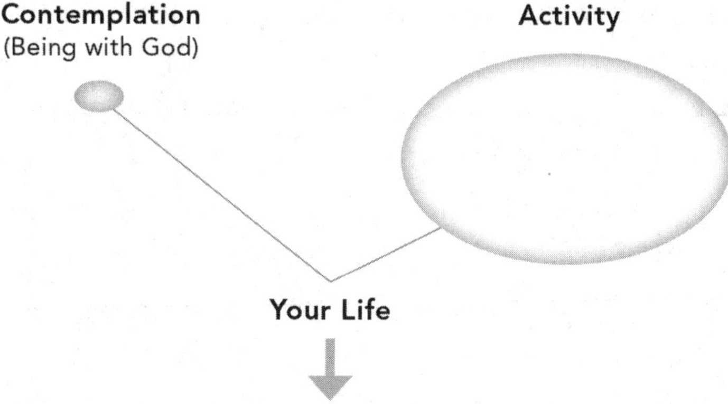

Now, using two circles like the ones in the diagram, draw your own diagram to illustrate how your activities (your doing) balance with your contemplative life (your being with God).[2]

3. The remaining sessions of the *EH Spirituality Course* will address ways we can make changes in our lives. At this point, what might be one or two simple steps you can take toward beginning to slow down your life and balance your two circles?

VIDEO: Closing Summary (8 minutes)

Watch the closing video summary for Session 1 and use the space provided to note anything that stands out to you.

NOTES

Between-Sessions Personal Study

SESSION 1

Read chapter 2 of the book *Emotionally Healthy Spirituality*, "Know Yourself That You May Know God." Use the space provided to note any insights or questions you might want to bring to the next group session.

Prayerfully read Week 1 of the devotional *Emotionally Healthy Spirituality Day by Day*, "The Problem of Emotionally Unhealthy Spirituality." Use the space provided to answer the Questions to Consider and/or to journal your thoughts each day.

Day 1 Questions to Consider:

How would you describe "what is secondary" in your life, the thing that might be "blocking the way" to experiencing God?

How could you make more room in your life for silence in order to listen to God?

Day 2 Questions to Consider:

What internal or external storm might God be sending into your life as a sign that something is not right spiritually?

How do you hear the words of the apostle John today: "Do not love the world or anything in the world" (1 John 2:15)?

Day 3 Questions to Consider:

In what way(s) has God put your life or plans "out of joint" so that you might depend on him?

What might be one way your "busyness" blocks you from listening and communing with the living God?

Day 4 Questions to Consider:

What things are "worrying" and "upsetting" you as you begin this day?

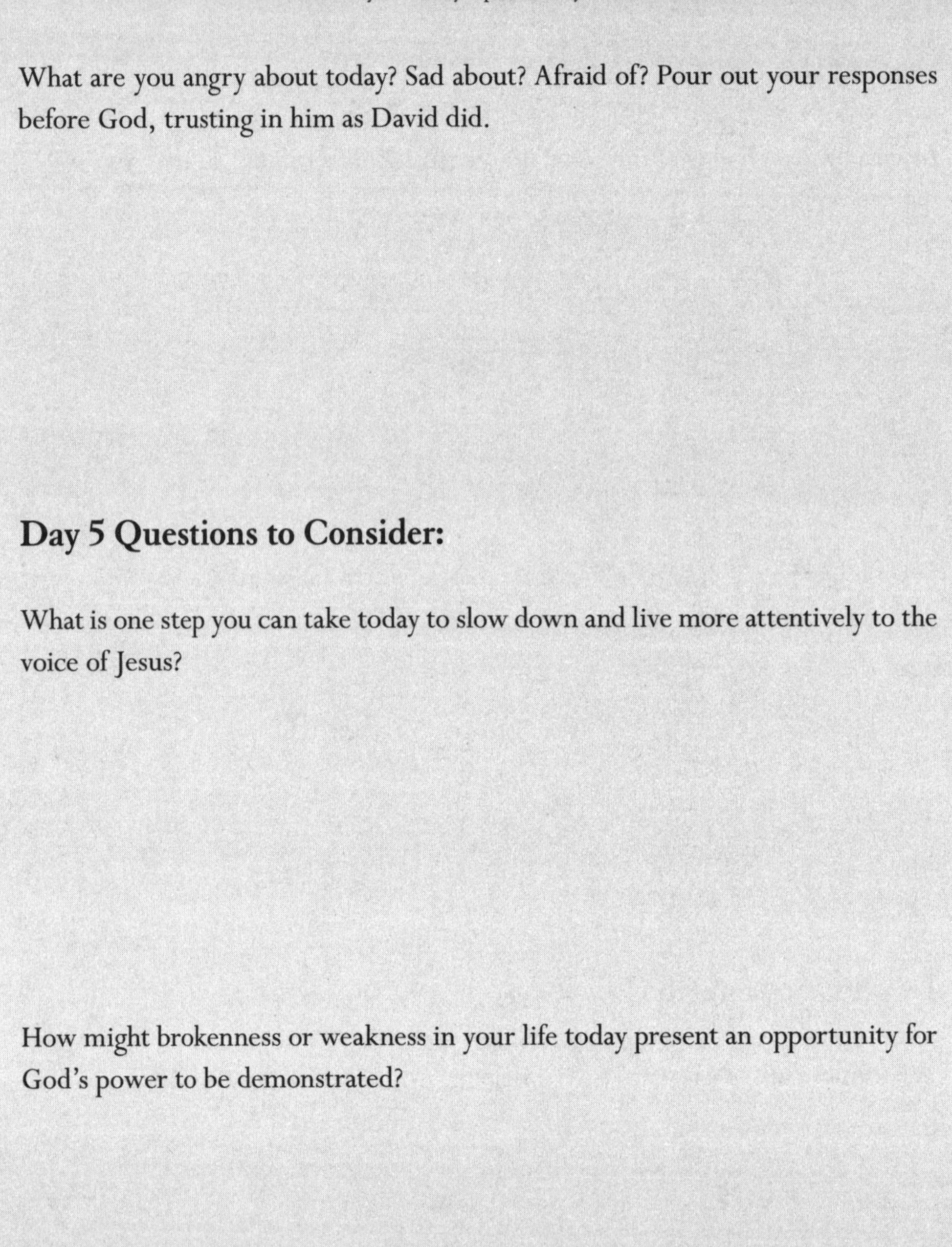

What are you angry about today? Sad about? Afraid of? Pour out your responses before God, trusting in him as David did.

Day 5 Questions to Consider:

What is one step you can take today to slow down and live more attentively to the voice of Jesus?

How might brokenness or weakness in your life today present an opportunity for God's power to be demonstrated?

SESSION 2

Know Yourself That You May Know God

Daily Office (10 minutes)

Do one of the Daily Offices from Week 2 of *Emotionally Healthy Spirituality Day by Day* to begin your session. **(Leaders, please see point number two in the "General Guidelines" on page 105.)**

Introduction (3 minutes)

Self-awareness is intricately related to our relationship with God. In fact, the challenge of Scripture to shed our old "false" self in order to live authentically in our new "true" self strikes at the very core of true spirituality.

In AD 500, Augustine wrote in *Confessions*, "How can you draw close to God when you are far from your own self?" He prayed: "Grant, Lord, that I may know myself that I may know thee."

In 1530, John Calvin wrote in his opening of the *Institutes of the Christian Religion*:

"Our wisdom . . . consists almost entirely of two parts: the knowledge of God and of ourselves. But as these are connected together by many ties, it is not easy to determine which of the two precedes and gives birth to the other."

The vast majority of us go to our graves without knowing who we are. Without being fully aware of it, we live someone else's life, or at least someone else's expectations for us. This does violence to ourselves, to our relationship with God, and ultimately to others.

In order to facilitate a sense of safety at each small group table, please turn to pages xi–xii as the "Guidelines for the Group" are read aloud.

Growing Connected (17 minutes)

1. *Day by Day* Debrief: God says: "Be still and know that I am God" (Psalm 46:10). This requires silence yet the practice of silence may be the weakest link in our discipleship today. What challenges are you experiencing as you begin and end your *EH Spirituality Day by Day* readings with silence? (7 minutes)

2. Describe your dream job. (10 minutes) This question often reveals seeds of how God has uniquely created you.

VIDEO: Know Yourself That You May Know God (10 minutes)

Watch the video teaching segment for Session 2. Use the space provided to note anything that stands out to you.

NOTES

Group Discussion (45 minutes)

Starters (10 minutes)

After the following paragraph is read aloud, complete question 1 on your own.

The journey of genuine transformation to emotionally healthy spirituality begins with a commitment to allow yourself to feel. Feelings are an essential part of our humanity and unique personhood as men and women created in God's image. Scripture reveals God as an emotional being who feels as a person. Having been created in his image, we also are created with the gift to feel and experience emotions. Some of us may have learned that feelings are not to be trusted; that they are dangerous and can lead us away from God's will for us. While it is true that we are not to be led by our emotions, they do serve a critical function in our discipleship and discernment of God's will.

1. Journal your response to the questions on the next page in the space provided. Your concern can be something from the past, present, or future. Consider prayerfully before the Lord, as David did in the Psalms, areas such as finances, health, relationships, work, etc. (5 minutes)

    - What are you angry about?

    - What are you sad about?

    - What are you anxious about?

    - What are you glad about?

2. Share in groups of two or three what it was like to journal your feelings? (5 minutes)

Bible Study: 1 Samuel 17:26–45 (35 minutes)

In this famous story, we will see a powerful picture of the common obstacles to living out of our true selves in Christ. As it begins, the army of Israel faced the great army of the Philistines. For forty days, the Philistine hero Goliath, described as nine feet tall and dressed in powerful weaponry, challenged any Israelite soldier to come out and fight him. When the Israelites saw him, however, "they all fled from him in great fear" (1 Samuel 17:24). We pick up the story after David hears, for the first time, Goliath's humiliating challenge to Israel's army. Listen carefully as the story from 1 Samuel 17:26–45 is read aloud.

> 26 David asked the men standing near him, "What will be done for the man who kills this Philistine and removes this disgrace from Israel? Who is this uncircumcised Philistine that he should defy the armies of the living God?"
>
> 27 They repeated to him what they had been saying and told him, "This is what will be done for the man who kills him."
>
> 28 When Eliab, David's oldest brother, heard him speaking with the men, he burned with anger at him and asked, "Why have you come down here? And with whom did you leave those few sheep in the wilderness? I know how conceited you are and how wicked your heart is; you came down only to watch the battle."
>
> 29 "Now what have I done?" said David. "Can't I even speak?" 30 He then turned away to someone else and brought up the same matter, and the men answered him as before. 31 What David said was overheard and reported to Saul, and Saul sent for him.
>
> 32 David said to Saul, "Let no one lose heart on account of this Philistine; your servant will go and fight him."
>
> 33 Saul replied, "You are not able to go out against this Philistine and fight him; you are only a young man, and he has been a warrior from his youth."
>
> 34 But David said to Saul, "Your servant has been keeping his father's sheep. When a lion or a bear came and carried off a sheep from the flock, 35 I went after it, struck it and rescued the sheep from its mouth. When it turned on me, I seized it by its hair, struck it and killed it. 36 Your servant has killed both the lion and the bear; this uncircumcised Philistine will be like one of them, because he has defied the armies of the living God. 37 The LORD who rescued me from the paw of the lion and the paw of the bear will rescue me from the hand of this Philistine."

Saul said to David, "Go, and the LORD be with you."

38 Then Saul dressed David in his own tunic. He put a coat of armor on him and a bronze helmet on his head. 39 David fastened on his sword over the tunic and tried walking around, because he was not used to them.

"I cannot go in these," he said to Saul, "because I am not used to them." So he took them off. 40 Then he took his staff in his hand, chose five smooth stones from the stream, put them in the pouch of his shepherd's bag and, with his sling in his hand, approached the Philistine.

41 Meanwhile, the Philistine, with his shield bearer in front of him, kept coming closer to David. 42 He looked David over and saw that he was little more than a boy, glowing with health and handsome, and he despised him. 43 He said to David, "Am I a dog, that you come at me with sticks?" And the Philistine cursed David by his gods. 44 "Come here," he said, "and I'll give your flesh to the birds and the wild animals!"

45 David said to the Philistine, "You come against me with sword and spear and javelin, but I come against you in the name of the LORD Almighty, the God of the armies of Israel, whom you have defied."

1. What are some of the strong, negative messages David receives from the people around him? (6 minutes)

    - From his own family (v. 28)

    - From Saul (vv. 33, 38)

    - From Goliath (vv. 41–45)

2. What feelings or pressures might you be experiencing if you were David (*ex.*: in response to an older sibling, a person in authority over you, or an intimidating person like Goliath)? (6 minutes)

3. Last week we observed Saul's false self (pretending to be someone on the outside that he is not on the inside, being afraid of what others think, not self-aware, not honest). Contrast this with the qualities of David's true self that we observe in this story as he stands up against powerful forces and pressures. (8 minutes)

4. Where in your life, or with whom, is it difficult to be your true self (*ex.*: to speak honestly, say "no," disagree with, or not be afraid of what others think)? (12 minutes)

Application (15 minutes)

Take time alone to prayerfully journal your responses to the questions below. (5 minutes)

1. What might it look like for you to take off armor that you are currently wearing that does not fit you?

2. Many of us are so unaccustomed to distinguishing our true self from our false self that it may seem difficult to know where to begin. Complete the following sentence: *What I am beginning to realize about myself is . . .*

Share your responses to questions 1 and 2 in groups of two or three. (10 minutes)

VIDEO: Closing Summary (8 minutes)

Watch the closing video summary for Session 2 and use the space provided to note anything that stands out to you.

NOTES

Between-Sessions Personal Study

SESSION 2

Read chapter 3 of the book *Emotionally Healthy Spirituality*, "Going Back in Order to Go Forward." Use the space provided to note any insights or questions you might want to bring to the next group session.

Prayerfully read Week 2 of the devotional *Emotionally Healthy Spirituality Day by Day*, "Know Yourself So That You May Know God." Use the space provided to answer the Questions to Consider and/or to journal your thoughts each day.

Day 1 Questions to Consider:

What might be one specific way that you give in to expectations of others rather than being faithful to what Jesus has for you?

What might be one false layer or bandage God is inviting you to remove today?

Day 2 Questions to Consider:

What do you think might be one of your "birthright" gifts from God that has been ignored in your life?

Where do you see yourself on Bernard's list of the four degrees of love?

Day 3 Questions to Consider:

What impresses you most about the story of Anthony's life?

What temptation(s) or trials do you find yourself in today that God may be using as a furnace to help develop your interior life?

Day 4 Questions to Consider:

What would it look like to respect yourself in light of your God-given limits?

What is one area of your inner person that the fire of God's presence might want to burn away (*ex.*: selfishness, greed, bitterness, impatience)?

Day 5 Questions to Consider:

How might it change your day today if you were to cease looking for human approval and begin seeking only the approval of God?

In what area of your life might you be living as a chicken when God, in reality, has made you an eagle?

SESSION 3

Going Back in Order to Go Forward

Daily Office (10 minutes)

Do one of the Daily Offices from Week 3 of *Emotionally Healthy Spirituality Day by Day* to begin your session. **(Leaders, please see point number two in the "General Guidelines" on page 105.)**

Introduction (1 minute)

Emotionally healthy spirituality involves embracing God's choice to birth us into a particular family, in a particular place, at a particular moment in history.

That choice to embrace our past grants us certain opportunities and gifts. It also hands us a certain amount of "emotional baggage" for our journey through life. For some of us this load is minimal; for others, it is a heavy burden to carry.

True spirituality frees us to live joyfully in the present. Living joyfully, however, requires going back in order to go forward. This process takes us to the very heart of spirituality and discipleship in the family of God—breaking free from the destructive sinful patterns of our past in order to live the life of love that God intends.

Growing Connected (10 minutes)

1. *Day by Day* Debrief: At the heart of this Course is nurturing your relationship with God, especially in silence and Scripture. How was your experience in practicing silence this week?

2. How did the family you grew up in do conflict and how did that impact you? (e.g., blaming, yelling, appeasing, criticizing, silent treatment, contempt, etc.).

VIDEO: Going Back in Order to Go Forward (12 minutes)

Watch the video teaching segment for Session 3. Use the space provided to note anything that stands out to you.

NOTES

Group Discussion (40 minutes)

Starters (7 minutes)

Our need to go back in order to go forward can be summed up in two essential biblical truths:

- The blessings and sins of our families going back two to three generations profoundly impact who we are today.
- Discipleship requires putting off the sinful patterns of our family of origin and relearning how to do life God's way in God's family.

What concerns or fears might you have in looking back at your family of origin to discern unhealthy patterns and themes? Explain.

Bible Study: Genesis 50:15–21 (33 minutes)

Read aloud the introductory paragraphs and then answer question 1.

The "family" is an emotional system of two to four generations who move through life together in different places at different times. When we are born into families, we inherit their ways of relating, their values, and their ways of living in the world. (Adopted children inherit not only birth family traits but draw on traits from their adoptive family.) Your family's story and your individual story cannot be separated.

Joseph is an excellent example of that reality. He was born into a complex, blended family where his father Jacob, Jacob's two wives, two concubines, and their children, all lived under one roof. Joseph was Jacob's favored son. As a result, his brothers grew jealous, leading them to sell Joseph to a merchant who took him to Egypt. The brothers never expected to hear from Joseph again. After he was sold, Joseph's life became tragically difficult. For the next ten to thirteen years, Joseph lived first as a slave, and later, as a prisoner falsely accused of rape.

1. Imagine yourself in Joseph's shoes sitting in a prison cell without any hope of freedom. What thoughts, feelings, or doubts might you have about your family? About yourself? About God? (7 minutes)

Now read aloud the next paragraph and Scripture passage before discussing the remaining questions.

Through God's miraculous intervention, Joseph was pulled from the pit of prison and made the second most powerful person in Egypt. Later, when his brothers came to Egypt for food during a famine in Israel, Joseph invited them to return for their father and live in Egypt—which they gladly did. But after Jacob died, the brothers began to worry. Read Genesis 50:15–21.

15 When Joseph's brothers saw that their father was dead, they said, "What if Joseph holds a grudge against us and pays us back for all the wrongs we did to him?" 16 So they sent word to Joseph, saying, "Your father left these instructions before he died: 17 'This is what you are to say to Joseph: I ask you to forgive your brothers the sins and the wrongs they committed in treating you so badly.' Now please forgive the sins of the servants of the God of your father." When their message came to him, Joseph wept.

18 His brothers then came and threw themselves down before him. "We are your slaves," they said.

19 But Joseph said to them, "Don't be afraid. Am I in the place of God? 20 You intended to harm me, but God intended it for good to accomplish what is now being done, the saving of many lives. 21 So then, don't be afraid. I will provide for you and your children." And he reassured them and spoke kindly to them.

2. What assumptions are the brothers making about Joseph in verse 15? (4 minutes)

3. Why do you think Joseph weeps (v. 17)? (4 minutes)

4. Joseph chooses to break the "normal" way his family deals with hurt feelings and conflict by forgiving his brothers. How might you have responded if you were in Joseph's position? (Be sure to honestly put yourself in Joseph's shoes.) (6 minutes)

5. Slowly, reread verses 19–21. Here we see Joseph's response to the enormous losses he experienced in his life. Carefully consider the different aspects of this response noted below.
   - "Don't be afraid."
   - "Am I in the place of God?"
   - "You intended to harm me, but God intended it for good."

   As you think about your own life story, and view of God, which one of these three statements speak the most to you and why? (8 minutes)

Application (25 minutes)

Complete question 1 on your own, using the chart on the next page. (10 minutes)

1. Joseph had a rich sense of being part of his family of origin and how it had shaped his life—both good and bad. We must honestly face the truths about our family of origin as well. Prayerfully complete the chart on the following page even if you have done a similar exercise before. We often receive new insights when we ponder and reflect on our family's impact on us at different times.

   - First, list the life messages you received from each of your parents or caretakers (*ex.*: Education is everything. You must achieve to be loved. Don't be sad. Don't make mistakes. Don't be weak. Always be nice. Don't assert yourself. Make a lot of money. Don't trust people).
   - Next, list any "earthquake" events that sent "aftershocks" into your extended family (*ex.*: abuse, premature or sudden deaths/losses, divorces, shameful secrets revealed, etc.).
   - Review the three separate boxes and summarize what messages about life/yourself/others you internalized. Then fill in the bottom box, "Cumulative messages I received."

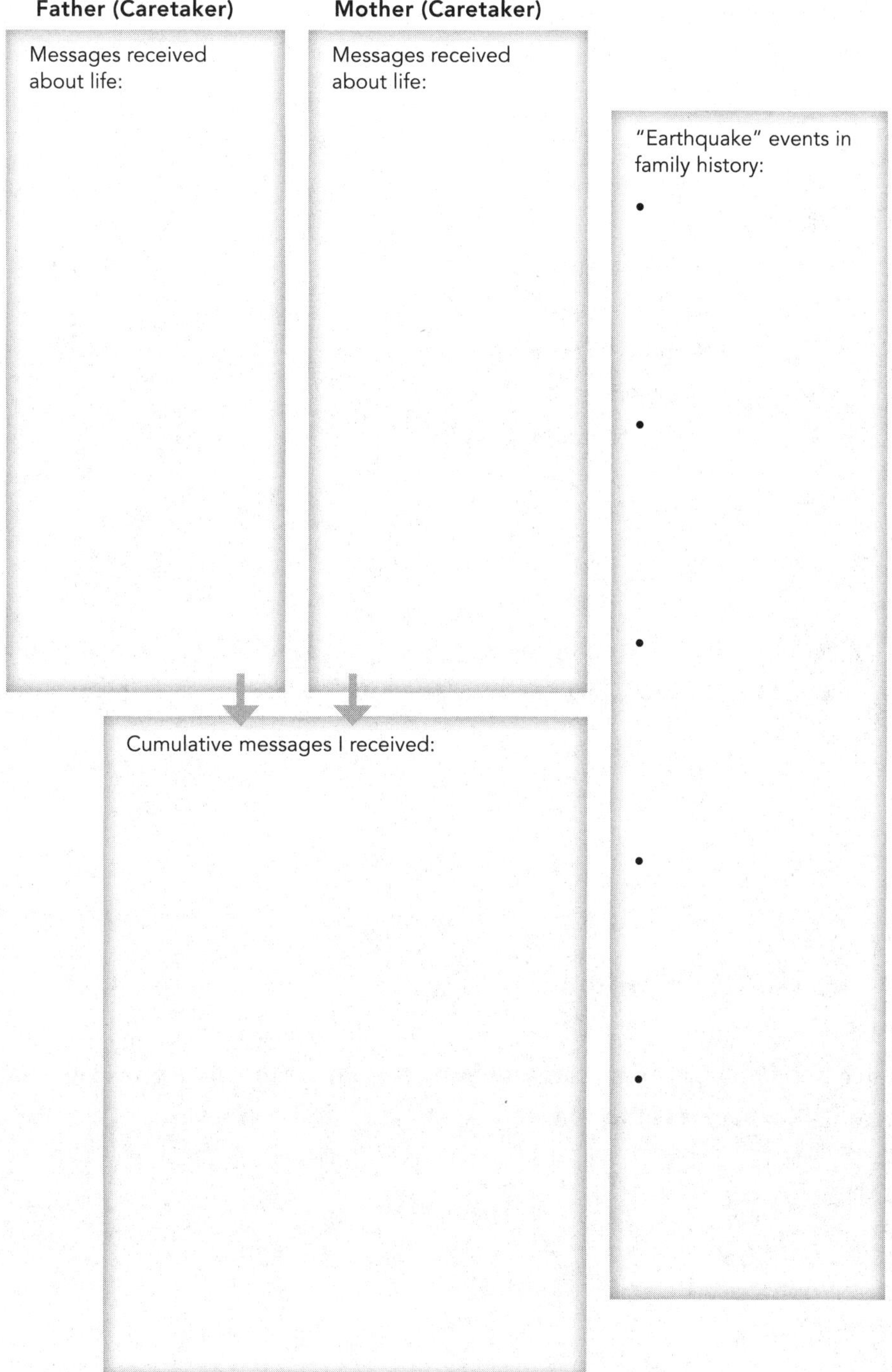
Father (Caretaker)
Messages received about life:
Mother (Caretaker)
Messages received about life:
"Earthquake" events in family history:
•
•
•
•
•
Cumulative messages I received:

2. Share with the group the message(s) you received. How do those messages compare with the messages below that reflect who you are in the new family of Jesus?

   - It is good that you exist.
   - You are lovable.
   - You are good enough.
   - You are a joy.
   - You have nothing left to prove.
   - Your needs are a delight.
   - You are allowed to make mistakes.

3. What might be one specific message from your family of origin that God has revealed to you today that you want to change as part of your "hard work of discipleship"?

VIDEO: Closing Summary (7 minutes)

Watch the closing video summary for Session 3 and use the space provided to note anything that stands out to you.

NOTES

Between-Sessions Personal Study

SESSION 3

Read chapter 4 of the book *Emotionally Healthy Spirituality*, "Journey through the Wall." Use the space provided to note any insights or questions you might want to bring to the next group session.

Prayerfully read Week 3 of the devotional *Emotionally Healthy Spirituality Day by Day*, "Going Back in Order to Go Forward." Use the space provided to answer the Questions to Consider and/or to journal your thoughts each day.

Day 1 Questions to Consider:

What invitation might God be offering to you out of the failures and pain of your past?

What heavy "raft" might you be carrying as you seek to climb the mountains God has placed before you?

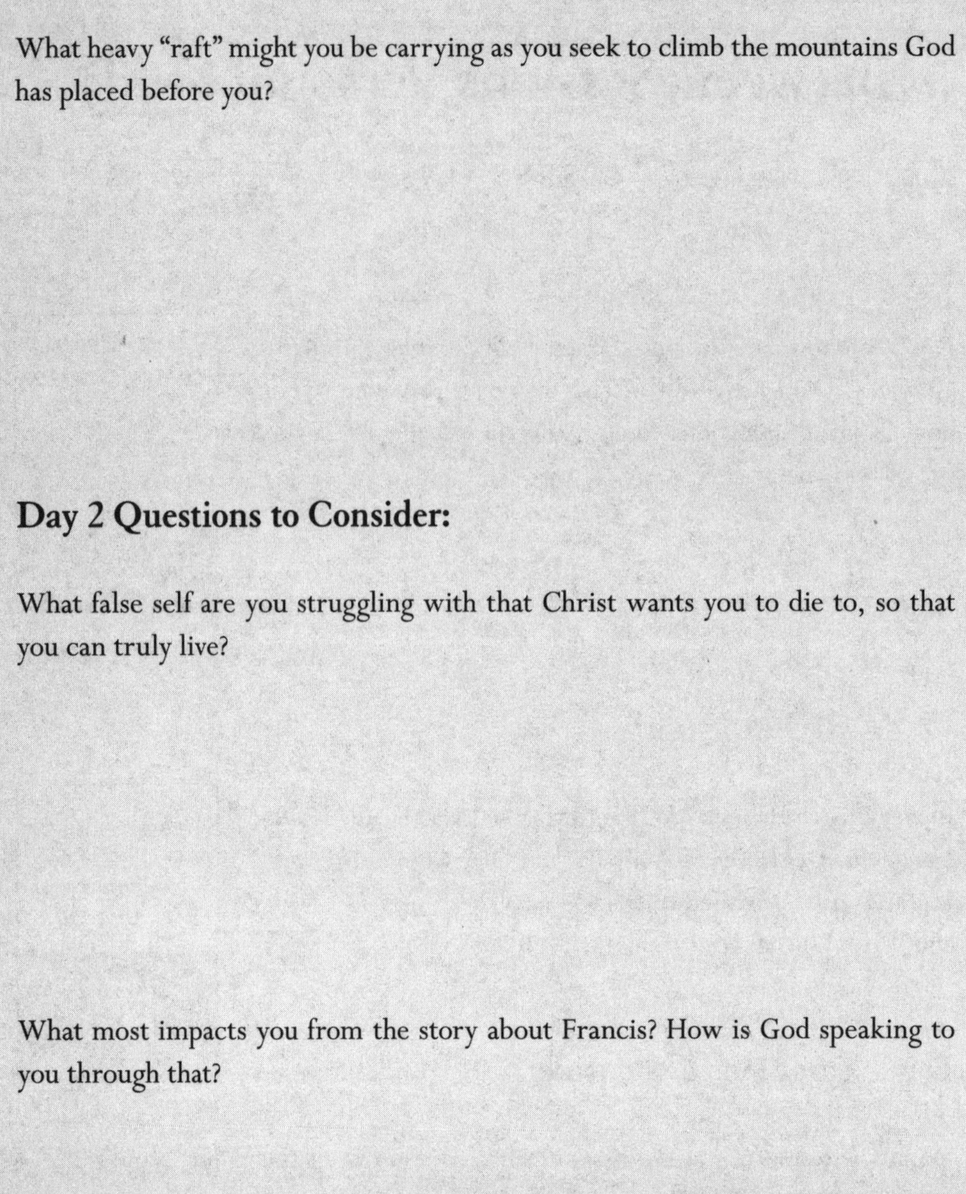

Day 2 Questions to Consider:

What false self are you struggling with that Christ wants you to die to, so that you can truly live?

What most impacts you from the story about Francis? How is God speaking to you through that?

Day 3 Questions to Consider:

What would it look like for you to surrender the pains of your past (mistakes, sins, setbacks, and disappointments) to God today?

What pains in your life are waiting to be acknowledged and grieved?

Day 4 Questions to Consider:

What space in the world (for which the past has prepared you) is waiting to be filled by you?

Can you name ways in which you learned the pain of others by suffering your own pain?

Day 5 Questions to Consider:

How might the words from Exodus 14:14–15—"The Lord will fight for you, you need only to be still" and "move on"—apply to you today?

In Psalm 131:1, David prays: "I do not concern myself with great matters or things too wonderful for me." How do you hear these words?

SESSION 4

Journey through the Wall

Daily Office (10 minutes)

Do one of the Daily Offices from Week 4 of *Emotionally Healthy Spirituality Day by Day* to begin your session. **(Leaders, please see point number two in the "General Guidelines" on page 105.)**

Introduction (1 minute)

Emotionally healthy spirituality requires that you go through the pain of the Wall—or, as the ancients called it, "the dark night of the soul." Just as a physical wall stops us from moving ahead, God sometimes stops us in our spiritual journey through a spiritual Wall in order to radically transform our character. Often, we are brought to the Wall by circumstances and crises beyond our control.

Regardless of how we get there, every follower of Jesus at some point will confront the Wall. Failure to understand and surrender to God's working in us at the Wall often results in great long-term pain, ongoing immaturity, and confusion. Receiving the gift of God in the Wall, however, transforms our lives forever.

Growing Connected (10 minutes)

1. *Day by Day* Debrief: Being still to know God more deeply (Psalm 46:10) is an invitation to surrender our will to God's will, as well as resting from our strivings and fears. How might silence enable you to surrender, relax, and enjoy God's rest in the midst of the anxieties you carry today?

2. Name one significant difficulty in your life that challenged your view (or expectations) of God.

VIDEO: Journey through the Wall (12 minutes)

Watch the video teaching segment for Session 4. Use the space provided to note anything that stands out to you.

NOTES

Group Discussion (50 minutes)

Starters (15 minutes)

Read aloud the following excerpt from the book *Emotionally Healthy Spirituality* before answering the question afterward.

> For most of us, the Wall appears through a crisis that turns our world upside down. It comes, perhaps, through a divorce, a job loss, the death of a close friend or family member, a cancer diagnosis, a disillusioning church experience, a betrayal, a shattered dream, a wayward child, a car accident, an inability to get pregnant, a deep desire to marry that remains unfulfilled, a spiritual dryness or a loss of joy in our relationship with God. We question ourselves, God, and the church. We discover for the first time that our faith does not appear to "work." We have more questions than answers as the very foundation of our faith feels like it is on the line. We don't know where God is, what he is doing, where he is going, how he is getting us there, or when this will be over. . . . It (the Wall) is not simply a one-time event that we pass through and get beyond. It appears to be something we return to as part of our ongoing relationship with God. (pages 101–102, *Updated Edition*)

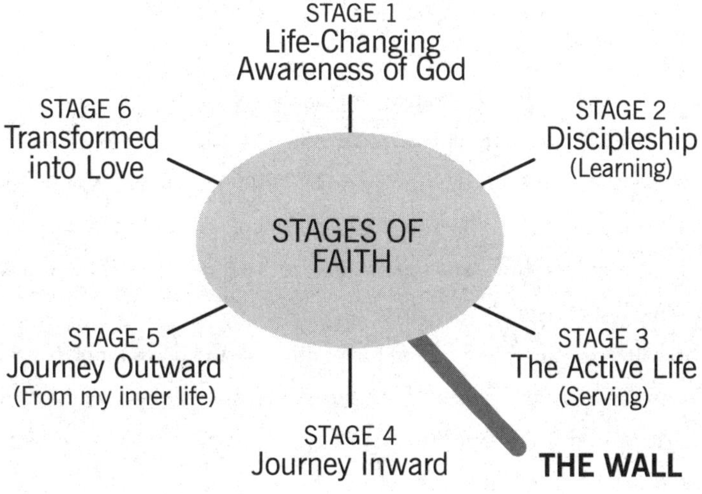

If you have been through a Wall, briefly share one way it impacted you and your view of God.

Bible Study: Genesis 22:1–14 (35 minutes)

Read aloud the introductory paragraph and Scripture passage, and then discuss the questions that follow.

Abraham, in his earthly pilgrimage with God, appeared to go through a number of Walls. His greatest one, however, came when God asked him to do the unthinkable—to kill his only son Isaac. Read Genesis 22:1–14:

> 1 Some time later God tested Abraham. He said to him, "Abraham!"
>
> "Here I am," he replied.
>
> 2 Then God said, "Take your son, your only son, whom you love—Isaac—and go to the region of Moriah. Sacrifice him there as a burnt offering on a mountain I will show you."
>
> 3 Early the next morning Abraham got up and loaded his donkey. He took with
> him two of his servants and his son Isaac. When he had cut enough wood for the
> burnt offering, he set out for the place God had told him about. 4 On the third day
> Abraham looked up and saw the place in the distance. 5 He said to his servants, "Stay
> here with the donkey while I and the boy go over there. We will worship and then
> we will come back to you."
>
> 6 Abraham took the wood for the burnt offering and placed it on his son Isaac,
> and he himself carried the fire and the knife. As the two of them went on together,
> 7 Isaac spoke up and said to his father Abraham, "Father?"
>
> "Yes, my son?" Abraham replied.
>
> "The fire and wood are here," Isaac said, "but where is the lamb for the burnt offering?"

8 Abraham answered, "God himself will provide the lamb for the burnt offering,
my son." And the two of them went on together.

9 When they reached the place God had told him about, Abraham built an altar
there and arranged the wood on it. He bound his son Isaac and laid him on the altar,
on top of the wood. 10 Then he reached out his hand and took the knife to slay his son.
11 But the angel of the LORD called out to him from heaven, "Abraham! Abraham!"

"Here I am," he replied.

12 "Do not lay a hand on the boy," he said. "Do not do anything to him. Now
I know that you fear God, because you have not withheld from me your son, your
only son."

13 Abraham looked up and there in a thicket he saw a ram caught by its horns.
He went over and took the ram and sacrificed it as a burnt offering instead of his
son. 14 So Abraham called that place The LORD Will Provide. And to this day it is
said, "On the mountain of the LORD it will be provided."

1. How would you hear the words in verse 2: "Take your son, your only son, whom you love . . . sacrifice him"? (3 minutes)

2. What aspects of "the dark night" might have been tormenting Abraham's soul as he bound his son Isaac and laid him on the altar? (*ex.*: weariness, sense of failure, defeat, emptiness, dryness, unbelief, guilt, disillusionment, abandonment by God) (4 minutes)

3. In light of this story, how is your image (or idea) of God challenged? (5 minutes)

4. What are some possible reasons you have a hard time accepting and moving through Walls? (Note: Speak in the "I.") (6 minutes)

5. In order to grow in Christ, every believer must go through Walls, or "dark nights of the soul." This is God's way of rewiring and "purging our affections and passions" that we might delight in his love and enter into a richer, fuller communion with him. In this way he frees us from unhealthy attachments, faulty images of who God is, and idolatries of the world. How might this larger perspective serve as an encouragement to you today? (8 minutes)

6. This Wall gave Abraham a revelation of God that would change him and his relationship with God forever. He came to know God as Provider in even the most desperate of situations (v. 14). How might this encourage you in any current Walls you are facing? (8 minutes)

Application (15 minutes)

Take about 5 minutes to complete question 1 on your own.

1. When God takes us through a Wall, we are changed. The following are four primary characteristics of life found on the other side of the Wall.

    - A greater level of brokenness
    - A greater appreciation for holy unknowing (mystery)
    - A deeper ability to wait on God
    - A greater detachment (from the world)

    Journaling can be a powerful tool to help clarify areas of life where God desires to bring transformation. It illuminates what is going on inside of us. Few tools get us to the "issue beneath the issue" like journaling.

    Choose one characteristic from the above list where you sense God is seeking to work in you now. Use the space provided to journal your thoughts and feelings regarding how God is birthing something new in you and/or helping you shed incomplete or immature ideas about him.

2. Form groups of two or three and share how you sense God might be working in you now.

VIDEO: Closing Summary (9 minutes)

Watch the closing video summary for Session 4 and use the space provided to note anything that stands out to you.

NOTES

Between-Sessions Personal Study

SESSION 4

Read chapter 5 of the book *Emotionally Healthy Spirituality*, "Enlarge Your Soul through Grief and Loss." Use the space provided to note any insights or questions you might want to bring to the next group session.

Prayerfully read Week 4 of the devotional *Emotionally Healthy Spirituality Day by Day*, "Journey through the Wall." Use the space provided to answer the Questions to Consider and/or to journal your thoughts each day.

Day 1 Questions to Consider:

What does it mean for you to trust in the slow work of God today?

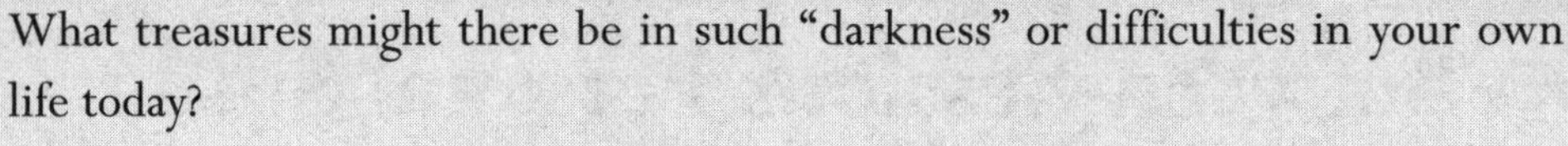

What treasures might there be in such "darkness" or difficulties in your own life today?

Day 2 Questions to Consider:

What might be some unhealthy attachments or "idols" God wants to remove from your life in order to lead you to deeper, richer communion with him?

What things or people are you rooting your identity in that God may want to dig up so that your identity might be replanted in him?

Day 3 Questions to Consider:

Have you experienced any "terrible" circumstances that (in time) actually turned out to be a rich blessing?

What words or phrases from the Richard Rohr quote most speak to you? Why?

Day 4 Questions to Consider:

How is God inviting you to wait on him today?

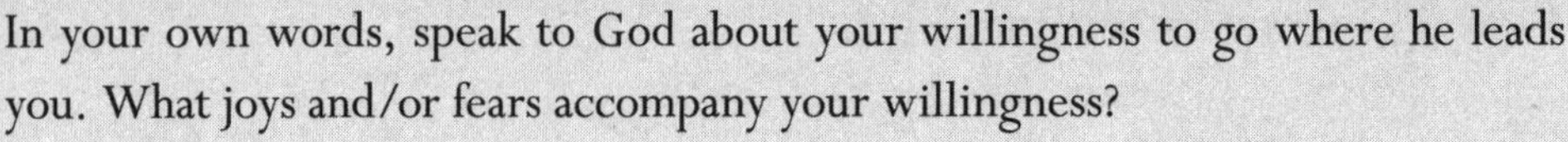

In your own words, speak to God about your willingness to go where he leads you. What joys and/or fears accompany your willingness?

Day 5 Questions to Consider:

What is one thing God might want you to unlearn today?

What words speak to you most from the prayer found in the midday/evening Office of Week 4? Why?

SESSION 5

Enlarge Your Soul through Grief and Loss

Daily Office (10 minutes)

Do one of the Daily Offices from Week 5 of *Emotionally Healthy Spirituality Day by Day* to begin your session. **(Leaders, please see point number two in the "General Guidelines" on page 105.)**

Introduction (1 minute)

Loss is a place where self-knowledge and powerful transformation can happen—if we have the courage to participate fully in the process.

We all face many "deaths" within our lives. Our culture routinely interprets these losses and griefs as alien invasions and interruptions to our "normal" lives. The choice is whether these deaths will be terminal (crushing our spirit and life) or will open us up to new possibilities and depths of transformation in Christ.

Growing Connected (13 minutes)

1. *Day by Day* Debrief: Through silence and stillness, God invites us to open our hearts to receive his unwavering love. On a scale of 1 to 5 (1 being the lowest and 5 the highest), where would you place your experience with silence as a means to receive God's love?

2. As you were growing up, how did you deal with your disappointments and sadnesses? Give one example.

VIDEO: Enlarge Your Soul through Grief and Loss (10 minutes)

Watch the video teaching segment for Session 5. Use the space provided to note anything that stands out to you.

NOTES

Group Discussion (50 minutes)

Starters (10 minutes)

Briefly share one loss you have experienced this past year. How has this loss impacted you?

Bible Study: Matthew 26:36–44 (25 minutes)

Read aloud the introductory paragraph and Scripture passage, and then discuss the questions that follow.

The end of Jesus' vibrant, popular, earthly life and ministry was an enormous loss to his disciples and followers. It was also, as we shall see, an enormous loss for Jesus. Read Matthew 26:36–44:

> 36 Then Jesus went with his disciples to a place called Gethsemane, and he said to
> them, "Sit here while I go over there and pray." 37 He took Peter and the two sons
> of Zebedee along with him, and he began to be sorrowful and troubled. 38 Then he
> said to them, "My soul is overwhelmed with sorrow to the point of death. Stay here
> and keep watch with me."
>
> 39 Going a little farther, he fell with his face to the ground and prayed, "My
> Father, if it is possible, may this cup be taken from me. Yet not as I will, but as
> you will."
>
> 40 Then he returned to his disciples and found them sleeping. "Couldn't you men
> keep watch with me for one hour?" he asked Peter. 41 "Watch and pray so that you
> will not fall into temptation. The spirit is willing, but the flesh is weak."
>
> 42 He went away a second time and prayed, "My Father, if it is not possible for
> this cup to be taken away unless I drink it, may your will be done."
>
> 43 When he came back, he again found them sleeping, because their eyes were
> heavy. 44 So he left them and went away once more and prayed the third time, saying
> the same thing.

1. Following is a list of common defenses we often use to protect ourselves from grief and loss. Checkmark the common defenses that you sometimes use: (5 minutes)

   - ☐ Denial
   - ☐ Minimizing (admitting something is wrong but in such a way that it appears less serious than it actually is)
   - ☐ Blaming others (or God)
   - ☐ "Over-spiritualizing"
   - ☐ Blaming oneself
   - ☐ Rationalizing (offering excuses and justifications)
   - ☐ Intellectualizing (giving analysis and theories to avoid personal awareness or difficult feelings)
   - ☐ Distracting
   - ☐ Becoming hostile
   - ☐ Medicating (with unhealthy addictions or attachments to numb our pain)

2. It is important for us to remember that Jesus was both fully human and fully God. Spend a few moments focusing on Jesus in verses 36–41. In contrast to the common defenses listed in question 1, what were some of the ways he dealt with and moved through his losses? (8 minutes)

3. What about Jesus' example of grieving most speaks to you about embracing your own grief and loss? (12 minutes)

Application (25 minutes)

Take 5–10 minutes on your own to journal your answers to questions 1–3 below.

1. Using the chart that follows, choose two or three age ranges of your life, and write down your significant losses during those years.

GRIEF CHART

Age (in years)	Losses/Disappointments Experienced	Your Response at the Time
3–12		
13–18		
19–25		
26–40		
41–60		
61+		

2. What was the experience of filling out the chart like for you? Did it reveal anything new to you? Explain. (10 minutes)

3. There are three core phases of biblical grieving: (1) Pay Attention; (2) Wait in the Confusing-In-Between; and (3) Let the Old Birth the New. Are there any losses you have not yet embraced where new life might still be waiting to be birthed? (10 minutes)

4. Break into groups of two or three people and share your answers to questions 2 and 3.

VIDEO: Closing Summary (8 minutes)

Watch the closing video summary for Session 5 and use the space provided to note anything that stands out to you.

NOTES

Between-Sessions Personal Study

SESSION 5

Read chapter 6 of the book *Emotionally Healthy Spirituality*, "Discover the Rhythms of the Daily Office and Sabbath." Use the space provided to note any insights or questions you might want to bring to the next group session.

Prayerfully read Week 5 of the devotional *Emotionally Healthy Spirituality Day by Day*, "Enlarge Your Soul through Grief and Loss." Use the space provided to answer the Questions to Consider and/or to journal your thoughts each day.

Day 1 Questions to Consider:

What does it mean for you to pray, "Yet not as I will, but as you will"?

How can you see God enlarging your soul through your losses?

Day 2 Questions to Consider:

In what ways is God bringing you to your knees before him through difficulties and setbacks in your life today?

What about Horatio Spafford and his relationship with Christ moves you the most?

Day 3 Questions to Consider:

What "road closed" sign is before you today that may be God's way of redirecting you to something new?

Name one or two limits God has placed in your life today as a gift.

Day 4 Questions to Consider:

What might it mean for you to mature by entering the painful reality of your losses rather than avoiding them?

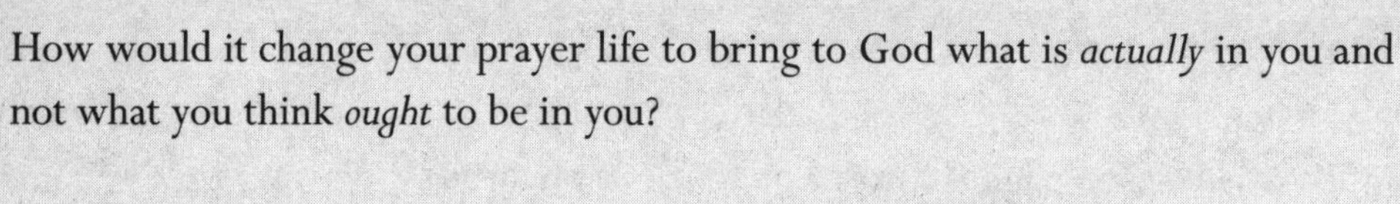

How would it change your prayer life to bring to God what is *actually* in you and not what you think *ought* to be in you?

Day 5 Questions to Consider:

In what way(s) are you tempted to spin or cover over your losses and miss God's deeper work in your interior?

How is God coming to you through the "mini-deaths" in your life now?

SESSION 6

Discover the Rhythms of the Daily Office and Sabbath

Daily Office (10 minutes)

Do one of the Daily Offices from Week 6 of *Emotionally Healthy Spirituality Day by Day* to begin your session. **(Leaders, please see point number two in the "General Guidelines" on page 105.)**

Introduction (1 minute)

Many of us are eager to develop our relationship with God. The problem, however, is that we can't seem to stop long enough to be with him. And if we aren't busy, we feel guilty that we are wasting time and not being productive. It is like being addicted—not to drugs or alcohol—but to tasks, work, and doing.

But God is offering us a way to deeply root our lives in him. This can be found in two ancient disciplines going back thousands of years—the Daily Office and Sabbath. When placed inside present-day Christianity, the Daily Office and

Sabbath are groundbreaking, countercultural acts that go against the grain of our fast-paced Western culture.

Stopping for the Daily Office and Sabbath is not meant to add another "to-do" to our already busy schedules. It is the resetting of our entire lives toward a new destination—God himself. These practices enable us to stay attuned to God's presence throughout our days and weeks.

Growing Connected (10 minutes)

1. *Day by Day* Debrief: Throughout church history, it has often been noted that silence is God's first language. When we are silent, we make room to hear God speak. In what new ways are you beginning to hear God through your silence and the *Day by Day* readings?

2. On a scale of 1 to 10 (1= least busy to 10 = very busy), how busy are you? And where on the scale would you like to be?

VIDEO: Discover the Rhythms of the Daily Office and Sabbath (12 minutes)

Watch the video teaching segment for Session 6. Use the space provided to note anything that stands out to you.

NOTES

Group Discussion (45 minutes)

Starters (10 minutes)

What is one practice you do on a daily/weekly basis that helps you stay connected to God?

Bible Study: Daniel 6:6–10; Exodus 20:1–17 (35 minutes)

Read aloud the introductory paragraph and the Daniel passage, and then answer questions 1–3. Then read aloud the Ten Commandments from Exodus 20:1–17 before answering questions 4–6.

After being forcibly removed from his country and home, Daniel was given a prestigious education and high-level job in government. The pressure on him to conform to the worldly, pagan values of Babylon was great. The following example gives us insight into one of the secrets of his faithful devotion to God. Read Daniel 6:6–10.

> 6 So these administrators and satraps went as a group to the king and said: "May King Darius live forever! 7 The royal administrators, prefects, satraps, advisers and governors have all agreed that the king should issue an edict and enforce the decree that anyone who prays to any god or human being during the next thirty days, except to you, Your Majesty, shall be thrown into the lions' den. 8 Now, Your Majesty, issue the decree and put it in writing so that it cannot be altered—in accordance with the law of the Medes and Persians, which cannot be repealed." 9 So King Darius put the decree in writing.
>
> 10 Now when Daniel learned that the decree had been published, he went home to his upstairs room where the windows opened toward Jerusalem. Three times a day he got down on his knees and prayed, giving thanks to his God, just as he had done before.

1. Reread verse 10 aloud. How do the words in this verse speak to you? (3 minutes)

2. How do you think this practice anchored Daniel in God and enabled him to resist the great pressure he was facing? (5 minutes)

3. What are the greatest obstacles preventing you from stopping to be with God once or twice a day? (8 minutes)

These are the Ten Commandments as recorded in Exodus 20:1–17:

1 And God spoke all these words:

2 "I am the LORD your God, who brought you out of Egypt, out of the land
of slavery.

3 "You shall have no other gods before me.

4 "You shall not make for yourself an image in the form of anything in heaven
above or on the earth beneath or in the waters below. . . .

7 "You shall not misuse the name of the LORD your God, for the LORD will not
hold anyone guiltless who misuses his name.

8 "Remember the Sabbath day by keeping it holy. 9 Six days you shall labor and
do all your work, 10 but the seventh day is a Sabbath to the LORD your God. On it
you shall not do any work, neither you, nor your son or daughter, nor your male or
female servant, nor your animals, nor any foreigner residing in your towns. 11 For
in six days the LORD made the heavens and the earth, the sea, and all that is in
them, but he rested on the seventh day. Therefore, the LORD blessed the Sabbath
day and made it holy.

12 "Honor your father and your mother, so that you may live long in the land
the LORD your God is giving you.

13 "You shall not murder.

14 "You shall not commit adultery.

15 "You shall not steal.

16 "You shall not give false testimony against your neighbor.

17 "You shall not covet your neighbor's house. You shall not covet your neighbor's wife, or his male or female servant, his ox or donkey, or anything that belongs to your neighbor."

4. Reread the fourth commandment in verses 8–11. Biblical Sabbaths are a 24-hour block of time each week with four characteristics that distinguish this time from a "day off."

    - **Stop:** "To stop" is built into the literal meaning of the Hebrew word. We have limits. God is on the throne running the world. We are called to let go and trust him.
    - **Rest:** Once we stop, we are called to rest from our work and our "doings."
    - **Delight:** We are to slow down so we can enjoy what we have been given.
    - **Contemplate:** We seek to see the invisible in the visible—to recognize the hidden ways the miracle of life is all around us in his gifts to us.

What 24-hour period might work for you at this phase of your journey to practice Sabbath? (5 minutes)

5. What do you need to stop that relates to your work—paid and unpaid? (5 minutes)

6. What activities, places, and/or people create rest and delight for you? (8 minutes)

Application (25 minutes)

1. Review the "Sabbath FAQs" on pages 68–71. Pick one question from among that list. In groups of two or three, discuss with one another the response to your question.

Sabbath FAQs

1. **Why do I need to keep Sabbath for a whole 24-hour period each week?**
God created us in his image for a rhythm of work and rest. When we violate that rhythm, we do violence to our own souls. Moreover, we are not defined by what we do or what we produce. We are defined by God's unconditional love for us in Christ Jesus. Therefore, we don't keep Sabbath to earn God's love. Rather, Sabbath is God's gift to keep us centered and rooted in that amazing reality. It is not an accident that this essential spiritual formation practice is found in the fourth commandment of the Ten Commandments.

2. **How do I go about deciding what specific activities are acceptable and unacceptable on the Sabbath?**
Reflect on the following questions as you sort out God's pathway for you:

   - What do I need to stop that relates to my work—paid and unpaid?
   - What activities create delight and rest for me?
   - How can I structure my day to cultivate a greater awareness of God in my life and in the world?
   - What might help me see God's goodness and miracles all around me today?

   Lynne Baab says, "Whatever we choose to do for Sabbath needs to give us rest and life over time. The challenge is discernment, experimenting to find what works for us and the people we love, what helps us catch our breath and remember who we are as God's beloved."

3. **Do I need a day-off and a Sabbath?**

You will need at least a half–day, or several hours, to prepare for Sabbath. Part of the Sabbath experience is the preparation time. What needs to happen before Sabbath starts so you (or your family) can experience true rest on the day itself? A basic list of what needs to get done before Sabbath starts might include getting the errands and chores of life done (e.g., food shopping, laundry, errands, cleaning the house, bringing closure to your work, final phone calls, paying bills). These things make Sabbath more restful and communicate the order and peace many of us long for.

4. **What do I do about my tendency to perfectionism?**

We don't ever get Sabbath "right." Sabbath is a day to let go of perfectionism and let God run the universe. Inconsistencies, bad choices, and learning from our mistakes are part of the point. Do your best to stop working, letting God worry about what you're not doing right, taking your focus off yourself so you can rest in him.

5. **Isn't Jesus our Sabbath-rest? Is this another works-righteousness?**

Jesus reinforced the gift of Sabbath amid all the abuses of his day. He reminds us, "The Sabbath was made for people, not people for the Sabbath" (Mark 2:27). To keep Sabbath is to exercise one's freedom, to declare oneself to be neither a tool to be "employed" nor a beast to be burdened. Sabbath-keeping is an invitation to rest because God rested. This rest serves as a sign of contemplation and abundance. God's gifts to humanity are so generous that we are able to rest. Our rest indicates that we depend completely on the God who redeemed us from sin, death, and evil.

6. **How do I cease from the work of parenting?**
   You cannot stop changing diapers, of course. But you can cease from tidying up, cooking, doing laundry, and running errands. You can do some things together as a family. You can hire a babysitter, so you and your spouse can get time alone. Or you can take time alone for yourself, leaving parenting to your spouse. Then, you take the children and give equal time to him/her.

7. **What do I do about my children who aren't interested in Sabbath?**
   The important thing to remember is that this is not a day of deprivation. Sabbath is to be a delight. Rather than simply taking things away, think about things you can add (e.g., special desserts, a movie, a creative family activity—depending on the ages of your children). It doesn't have to be a forced family day. If your children are older, they are going to naturally want to connect with their friends. That is okay. You will go through many transitions in keeping Sabbath, depending on your children's ages and temperaments. But, whenever possible, remember this is a wonderful opportunity to build rhythm, intentionality, and sacred traditions into your family.

8. **What about sports and extracurricular activities my children may be involved in?**
   There may be some activities you want to eliminate because of the stress involved. But there may be others (e.g., if your child loves soccer) that you will continue, but you will do so in a different spirit. You may go to the soccer game but you are doing it without multitasking, talking on the phone, reading emails, or reading work-related paperwork at halftime or during time outs. You can focus on enjoying the game, other parents, or the very gift of the human body able to participate in athletics.

9. **How, like Jesus, can we exercise compassion on the Sabbath without turning it into work?**
   The Jews have long believed that showing compassion on the Sabbath reflects the glorious abundance of the day. We rest from work in order to turn our hearts toward God, and God is always concerned with human need. When we stop for Sabbath, it may happen that we become more attentive to the problems of the world around us. This ultimately leads us to show more, not less, compassion. Maybe the Good Samaritan was on his Sabbath! Just be careful that it is not a "should." Rejoice in small acts of caring, allowing them to connect us to our compassionate God.

10. **Which day is the Sabbath? Sunday or Saturday? I have heard different views.**
    Paul addresses this very issue in the Jew/Gentile/multicultural church in Romans 14:1–8. He writes: "One man considers one day more sacred than another; another considers every day alike. Each one should be fully convinced in his own mind. He who regards one day as special, does so to the Lord . . ." I believe the key principle is keeping a rhythm for the same day of the week each week. Doing it around the Sunday gathering of worship is clearly best when possible, I believe, as this is part of our contemplation.

11. **Can I serve at church as a volunteer? Should I stop?**
    Yes, you can serve in your community. Except for a very, very few, our work is not at our church. We work as secretaries, social workers, teachers, lawyers, accountants, moms/dads at home, students, etc. Serving in our church community is not our job. Hopefully, there is delight in serving Christ as a children's worker, usher, greeter, etc. It is also important to remember that showing mercy and compassion was the missing element Jesus brought back into God's original intention of Sabbath-keeping. Treating people like Christ—whether children, youth, or adults—is the heart of what we seek to do in our churches.

2. In the space provided, take a few minutes to journal one small step you can take to begin to incorporate Sabbath as a spiritual formation practice (or to broaden and deepen your Sabbath if you have already begun practicing Sabbath).

3. Share that step with one other person.

VIDEO: Closing Summary (8 minutes)

Watch the closing video summary for Session 6 and use the space provided to note anything that stands out to you.

NOTES

Between-Sessions Personal Study

SESSION 6

Read chapter 7 of the book *Emotionally Healthy Spirituality*, "Grow into an Emotionally Mature Adult." Use the space provided to note any insights or questions you might want to bring to the next group session.

Prayerfully read Week 6 of the devotional *Emotionally Healthy Spirituality Day by Day*, "Discover the Rhythms of the Daily Office and Sabbath." Use the space provided to answer the Questions to Consider and/or to journal your thoughts each day.

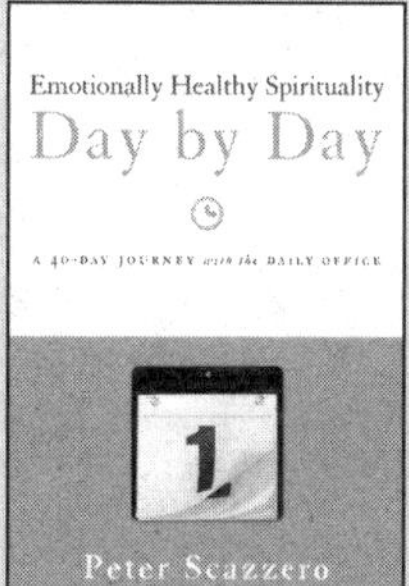

Day 1 Questions to Consider:

Pause and consider your day. What "seeds" from God might be coming to you that you don't want to miss?

How do you hear the invitation to "stop and surrender to God in trust" today?

Day 2 Questions to Consider:

When can you set aside some time for extended, uninterrupted silence to hear God?

How might you be busier than God requires?

Day 3 Questions to Consider:

What keeps you from silence?

How do the rhythms you see in nature (spring, summer, fall, winter, day, night) speak to you about the kind of rhythms you desire for your own life?

Day 4 Questions to Consider:

What is your greatest fear in stopping for a 24-hour period each week?

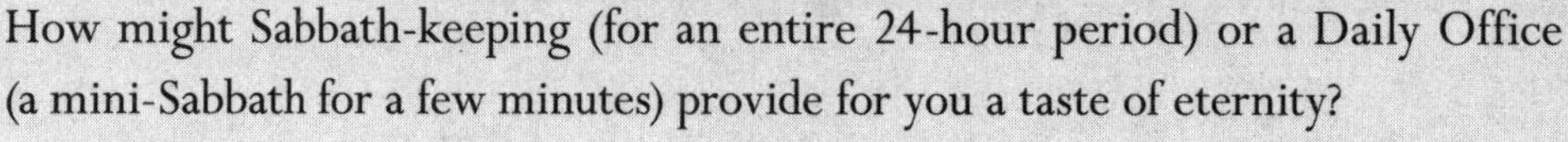

How might Sabbath-keeping (for an entire 24-hour period) or a Daily Office (a mini-Sabbath for a few minutes) provide for you a taste of eternity?

Day 5 Questions to Consider:

How will you allow God to lead you to the "quiet waters" of rest this week so that you experience his unconditional love and acceptance?

How might the truth that God doesn't want to use you, but to enjoy you, give you a vision for celebrating Sabbath?

SESSION 7

Grow into an Emotionally Mature Adult

Daily Office (10 minutes)

Do one of the Daily Offices from Week 7 of *Emotionally Healthy Spirituality Day by Day* to begin your session. **(Leaders, please see point number two in the "General Guidelines" on page 105.)**

Introduction (1 minute)

The goal of the Christian life is to love well. Jesus was aware that true spirituality included not only loving God, but also the skill of loving others maturely.

Growing into an emotionally mature Christian person includes experiencing each individual, ourselves included, as sacred, or as Martin Buber put it, as a "Thou" rather than an "It." Becoming emotionally mature requires learning, practicing, and integrating such skills as speaking respectfully, listening with empathy, negotiating conflict fairly, and uncovering the hidden expectations we have of others . . . just to name a few.

As we will see in today's Bible study on the parable of the Good Samaritan, both self-respect and compassion for others are part of a life rooted in "I-Thou" relating.

Growing Connected (10 minutes)

1. *Day by Day* Debrief: We are hard-wired by God, not just for work and activity, but for stopping and resting in order to nurture our relationship with him. What are you discovering about the importance of having a rhythm of stopping in order to be still and know that he is God (Psalm 46:10).

2. As a group, brainstorm two lists (on a whiteboard, if one is available): qualities that describe emotional immaturity and qualities that describe emotional maturity. As you think about these qualities, consider how we treat/view ourselves and how we treat/view other people.

Emotional Immaturity	Emotional Maturity

VIDEO: Grow into an Emotionally Mature Adult (10 minutes)

Watch the video teaching segment for Session 7. Use the space provided to note anything that stands out to you.

NOTES

Group Discussion (45 minutes)

Starters (7 minutes)

Why do you think we can be committed and "growing" in Christ and yet not be growing in our ability to be "prayerfully present" or loving toward others?

Bible Study: Luke 10:25–37 (35 minutes)

Read the introductory paragraph and Scripture passage, and then discuss the questions that follow.

Who can hear a story on the news about someone getting mugged, robbed, stripped naked, and left for dead in an alleyway without being affected? These real-life stories also happened in the days of Jesus. And Jesus told a parable recorded in Luke 10:25–37 that imagines one such disturbing story—with an unusual twist.

> 25 On one occasion an expert in the law stood up to test Jesus. "Teacher," he asked,
> "what must I do to inherit eternal life?"
>
> 26 "What is written in the Law?" he replied. "How do you read it?"
>
> 27 He answered, "'Love the Lord your God with all your heart and with all your
> soul and with all your strength and with all your mind'; and, 'Love your neighbor
> as yourself.'"
>
> 28 "You have answered correctly," Jesus replied. "Do this and you will live."
>
> 29 But he wanted to justify himself, so he asked Jesus, "And who is my neighbor?"
>
> 30 In reply Jesus said: "A man was going down from Jerusalem to Jericho, when
> he was attacked by robbers. They stripped him of his clothes, beat him and went
> away, leaving him half dead. 31 A priest happened to be going down the same road,
> and when he saw the man, he passed by on the other side. 32 So too, a Levite, when
> he came to the place and saw him, passed by on the other side. 33 But a Samaritan, as
> he traveled, came where the man was; and when he saw him, he took pity on him.
> 34 He went to him and bandaged his wounds, pouring on oil and wine. Then he put
> the man on his own donkey, brought him to an inn and took care of him. 35 The next
> day he took out two denarii and gave them to the innkeeper. 'Look after him,' he
> said, 'and when I return, I will reimburse you for any extra expense you may have.'
>
> 36 "Which of these three do you think was a neighbor to the man who fell into
> the hands of robbers?"
>
> 37 The expert in the law replied, "The one who had mercy on him."
>
> Jesus told him, "Go and do likewise."

1. According to Martin Buber, the great Jewish theologian, we treat people as an "It" when we use them as means to an end or as objects. We treat people as a "Thou" when we recognize each person as a separate human being made in God's image and treat them with dignity and respect.[1] If you were the priest

or Levite, what are some of the reasons you may have passed by this man and treated him as an "It" instead of a "Thou"? (3 minutes)

2. Look back at verses 31–33. What did the Samaritan see and feel that the priest and Levite did not? (3 minutes)

3. On your own, journal your thoughts on the following questions for two minutes. Then have one or two volunteers share their responses. (6 minutes)

    - Can you think of a time when you were seen in a negative light, treated as inferior, or passed over as invisible? How did it feel?

    - Who have you been taught not to see (i.e., to treat as an "It")?

4. Reread verses 33–36. The Samaritan's compassion led him to stop and help the hurting man. At the same time, how did he demonstrate awareness of his limits? (6 minutes)

5. What are some of your challenges when it comes to loving your neighbor and loving yourself? (8 minutes)

6. In light of how God is coming to you through this study, how do you hear the words in verse 37 to "go and do likewise"? (9 minutes)

Application[2] (25 minutes)

Read aloud the introductory paragraphs below. Answer questions 1 and 2 on your own. Then, in groups of two or three, answer question 3 and close in prayer.

One way of growing in the area of loving others well, and treating ourselves and others as a "Thou," is to understand how we manage our expectations in relationships. We get a glimpse of this, for example, in how the Good Samaritan managed expectations with the innkeeper.

EXPECTATIONS are ASSUMPTIONS about what someone SHOULD do. Every time we make an assumption about someone without checking it out, it is likely we are treating them as an "It" and not a "Thou." Why? We are jumping to conclusions without having checked out the assumption. Consider how you feel when someone is angry with you because you didn't fulfill their expectations, yet they never communicated this expectation to you. They simply assumed you should know.

Unmet and unclear expectations can create havoc in our places of employment, classrooms, friendships, dating relationships, marriages, sports teams, families, and churches. We expect other people to know what we want before we say it. The problem with most expectations is that they are:

- **Unconscious:** We may have expectations we're not even aware of until we are disappointed by someone.
- **Unrealistic:** We may develop unrealistic expectations by watching TV, movies, or other people/resources that give false impressions.
- **Unspoken:** We may have never told our spouse, friend, or employee what we expect, yet we are angry when our "expectations" are not met.
- **Un-agreed upon:** We may have had our own thoughts about what was expected, but those thoughts were never agreed upon by the other person.

Expectations are only valid when they have been mutually agreed upon.

1. Think of a recent, simple expectation that went unmet and made you angry or disappointed. (*Ex.*: I expected my husband to accompany me to my office party this past weekend; I expected to socialize with members of my small group outside the meeting times; I expected my teenagers to put their dirty dishes in the dishwasher; I expected my boss to give me at least a 5 percent cost of living raise last year.) Write yours down and then go on to question 2.

2. Now compare that unmet expectation with the inventory questions below:

    - **Conscious:** Were you conscious (aware) you had this expectation?

    - **Realistic:** Is the expectation realistic regarding the other person?

    - **Spoken:** Have you clearly spoken the expectation to them or do you just think "they should know"?

    - **Agreed upon:** Has the other person agreed to the expectation?

Remember this principle: Expectations are only valid when they have been mutually agreed upon. These are the expectations we have a right to expect.

3. Break into groups of two or three and respond to the following two questions:

    - What did you discover about your expectations?

    - What step(s) can you take to make your expectations conscious, spoken, realistic, and agreed upon so that you are relating in an "I-Thou" way?

VIDEO: Closing Summary (7 minutes)

Watch the closing video summary for Session 7 and use the space provided to note anything that stands out to you.

NOTES

Between-Sessions Personal Study

SESSION 7

Read chapter 8 of the book *Emotionally Healthy Spirituality*, "Go the Next Step to Develop a 'Rule of Life.'" Use the space provided to note any insights or questions you might want to bring to the next group session.

Prayerfully read Week 7 of the devotional *Emotionally Healthy Spirituality Day by Day*, "Grow into an Emotionally Mature Adult." Use the space provided to answer the Questions to Consider and/or to journal your thoughts each day.

Day 1 Questions to Consider:

What is one step you can take to place yourself (with all your flaws) in the hands of Jesus, inviting him to mold you into a spiritually and emotionally mature disciple?

How can you "practice the presence of people," within an awareness of his presence today?

Day 2 Questions to Consider:

Which words from Henri Nouwen's quotation about the prodigal son speak to you?

What is the biggest challenge you face in being still before the Lord?

Day 3 Questions to Consider:

How can you begin to see Jesus Christ in the people you meet this week?

Take a few moments and consider the people you will encounter today. What might it look like for you to slow down and treat each one as a "Thou" rather than an "It"?

Day 4 Questions to Consider:

What sometimes distracts you from seeing the people you are with as they really are?

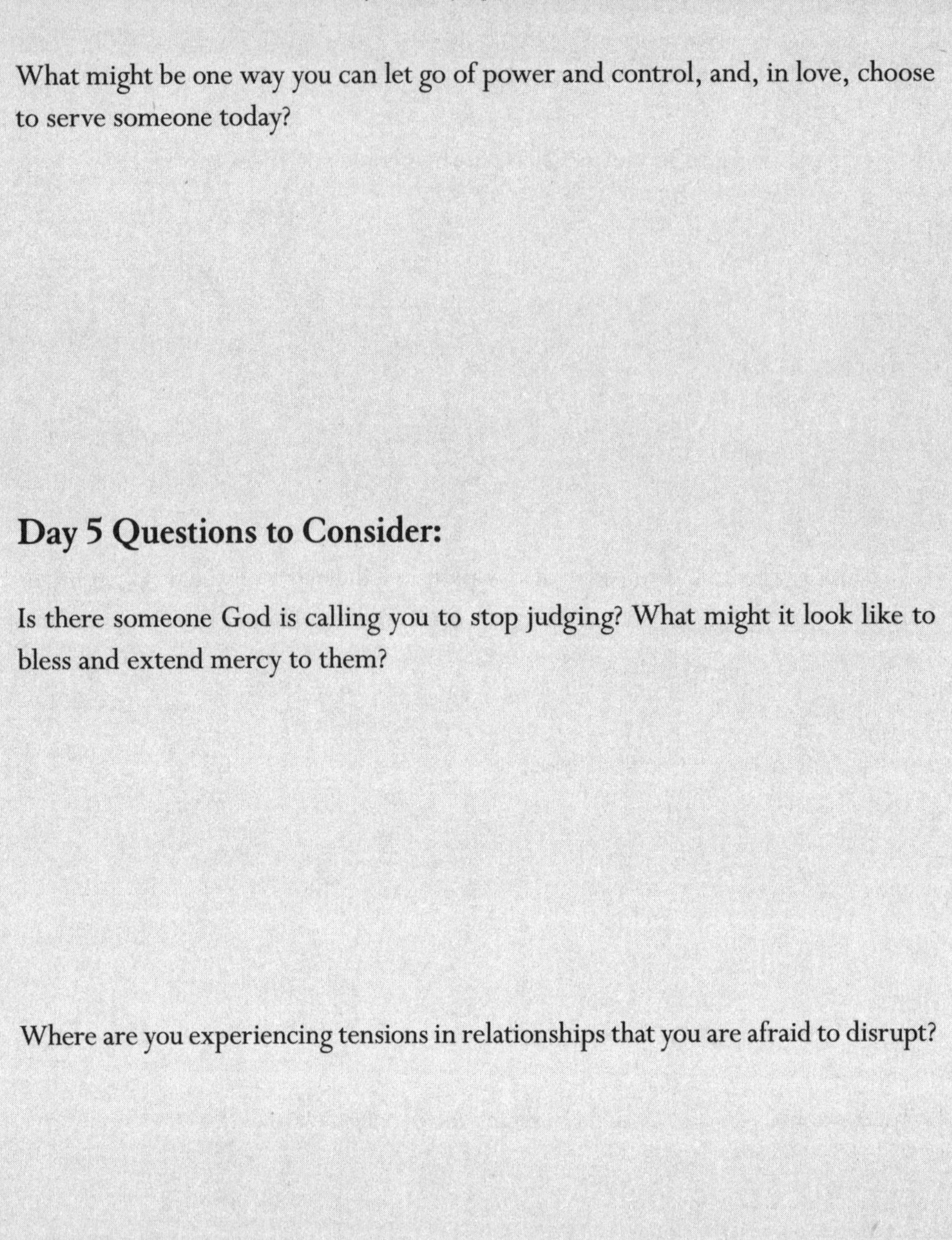

What might be one way you can let go of power and control, and, in love, choose to serve someone today?

Day 5 Questions to Consider:

Is there someone God is calling you to stop judging? What might it look like to bless and extend mercy to them?

Where are you experiencing tensions in relationships that you are afraid to disrupt?

SESSION 8

Go the Next Step to Develop a "Rule of Life"

Daily Office (10 minutes)

Do one of the Daily Offices from Week 8 of *Emotionally Healthy Spirituality Day by Day* to begin your session. **(Leaders, please see point number two in the "General Guidelines" on page 105.)**

Introduction (1 minute)

If we are to nurture a heart that treats every person, ourselves included, as a "Thou" instead of "It," we need to be intentional about our lives. By ordering our lives to contemplate the love of Christ and to receive the love of Christ, we will be able to give the love of Christ away to others. In this way, he transforms our lives into a gift to our families, friends, coworkers, and communities.

The problem again, however, is our busyness and lack of intentionality. Often, we find ourselves unfocused, distracted, and spiritually adrift. Few of us have a conscious plan for intentionally developing our spiritual lives.

Nurturing a growing spirituality in our present-day culture calls for a thoughtful, conscious, purposeful plan. To do this well requires us to uncover another ancient buried treasure—a "Rule of Life."

Growing Connected (12 minutes)

1. *Day by Day Debrief*: The goal of stopping for the Daily Office is to increase our awareness of God's presence throughout the entire day—in the midst of our activities. In what new ways, small or large, are you beginning to experience this greater awareness of God during the day as you practice the Daily Office?

2. What has impacted you most from this Course? (e.g., themes from one of the sessions, your table group, silence, the Daily Office, etc.) Briefly explain.

- The Problem of Emotionally Unhealthy Spirituality
  (Saul—living out of a false self and not cultivating his relationship with God)
- Know Yourself That You May Know God
  (David—courageously living out of his true self)
- Going Back in Order to Go Forward
  (Joseph—transformed by a very difficult past)
- Journey through the Wall
  (Abraham—trusting God in a "dark night of the soul")
- Enlarge Your Soul through Grief and Loss
  (Jesus in Gethsemane—embracing God's will)
- Discover the Rhythms of the Daily Office and Sabbath
  (Daniel—anchoring himself in God)
- Grow into an Emotionally Mature Adult
  (The Good Samaritan—modeling an "I-Thou" heart to others)

VIDEO: Go the Next Step to Develop a "Rule of Life" (11 minutes)

Watch the video teaching segment for Session 8. Use the space provided to note anything that stands out to you.

NOTES

Group Discussion (25 minutes)

Starters (10 minutes)

A Rule of Life finds its roots from the early centuries of the church as men and women formed communities and organized their daily life around an intentional and purposeful plan to grow and mature spiritually. They called this plan a Rule of Life.

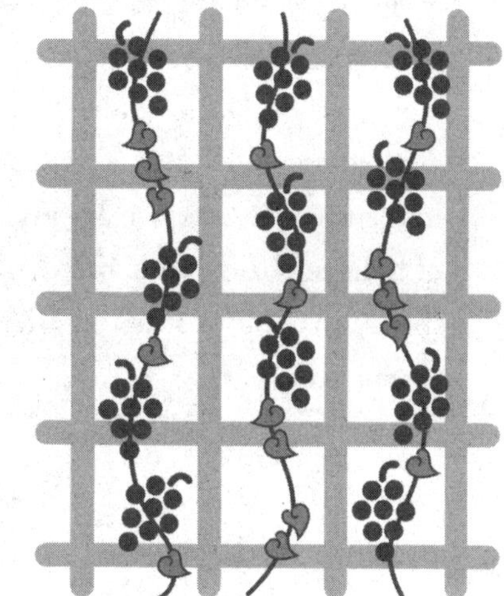

The word *rule* comes from the Greek word for "trellis." A trellis is a tool that enables a grapevine to get off the ground and grow upward, becoming more fruitful and productive. In the same way, a Rule of Life is a trellis that helps us abide in Christ and become more fruitful spiritually.[1]

A simple, clear definition of a Rule of Life is that it is an intentional, conscious plan to keep God at the center of everything we do.

How intentional are you about engaging in spiritual practices and rhythms that enable you to pay attention to God in everything you do? Use a scale of 1–10, with 1 being "not at all intentional" and 10 being "completely intentional." What number best describes where you are now? What numbers describes where you would like to be?

Bible Study: Acts 2:42–47 (15 minutes)

The book of Acts describes for us the Rule of Life of the first Christian community. Read Acts 2:42–47, and then discuss the questions that follow.

> [42] They devoted themselves to the apostles' teaching and to fellowship, to the breaking
> of bread and to prayer. [43] Everyone was filled with awe at the many wonders and signs
> performed by the apostles. [44] All the believers were together and had everything in
> common. [45] They sold property and possessions to give to anyone who had need.
> [46] Every day they continued to meet together in the temple courts. They broke
> bread in their homes and ate together with glad and sincere hearts, [47] praising God
> and enjoying the favor of all the people. And the Lord added to their number daily
> those who were being saved.

1. In the book of Acts, we are given a window into the life of the first community of believers soon after the coming of the Holy Spirit at Pentecost when three thousand people came to faith in Christ. What speaks to you from this passage? (6 minutes)

2. Based on this one passage, how would you describe this community's Rule of Life? Describe the activities/disciplines they intentionally used to grow and mature in Christ. (6 minutes)

Application (48 minutes)

As you craft your Rule of Life, consider the diagram below.

We were created to receive and give the love of God. *Emotionally Healthy Spirituality* (Part 1) was created to help us receive and give this love in our daily lives.

As you reflect on the seven session topics from this Course, journal your responses to questions 1–6 prayerfully. (15 minutes.)

1. Which session(s) have you found most helpful?

2. What positive impact are you experiencing now in your life and/or relationships as a result of having taken this Course?

3. What might be 1–3 truths or applications that God is inviting you to intentionally focus on during the next three months? Write it/them down in the chart that follows. We recommend that you start with only one to three. When you begin to make progress in these, then you can move on to others.

Truth/Application	Your Next Step	Resources/Support You May Need

4. What obstacles come to mind when you think of implementing these new learnings from God into your life? What obstacles might you face if you don't?

5. What one or two steps could you take to overcome the obstacles you just identified?

6. After your time alone, get into groups of two, and share what you discovered. (10 minutes)

Final Group Time (25 minutes)

Share your answers to the following questions.

1. Finish the following sentence stem:

   As a result of this course, I am beginning to realize . . .

2. What is one hope or dream you have as you go forward from this Course?

VIDEO: Closing Summary (7 minutes)

Watch the closing video summary for Session 8 and use the space provided to note anything that stands out to you.

NOTES

Personal Study for the Coming Days

SESSION 8

Prayerfully read Week 8 of the devotional *Emotionally Healthy Spirituality Day by Day*, "Go the Next Step to Develop a 'Rule of Life.'" Use the space provided to answer the Questions to Consider and/or to journal your thoughts each day.

Day 1 Questions to Consider:

What is your plan, in the midst of your busy day, for not leaving the nurture of your interior life with God to chance?

How and why do you think finding time alone with God in silence might "teach you everything"?

Day 2 Questions to Consider:

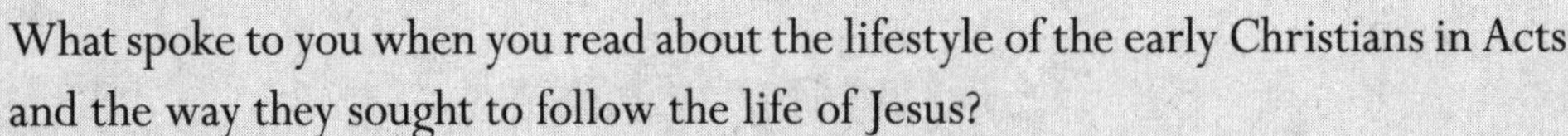

What spoke to you when you read about the lifestyle of the early Christians in Acts and the way they sought to follow the life of Jesus?

Where can you find the time in your week to "gaze on the infinite beauty of God"?

Day 3 Questions to Consider:

What difference might it make if you were to practice "building open spaces" into your life?

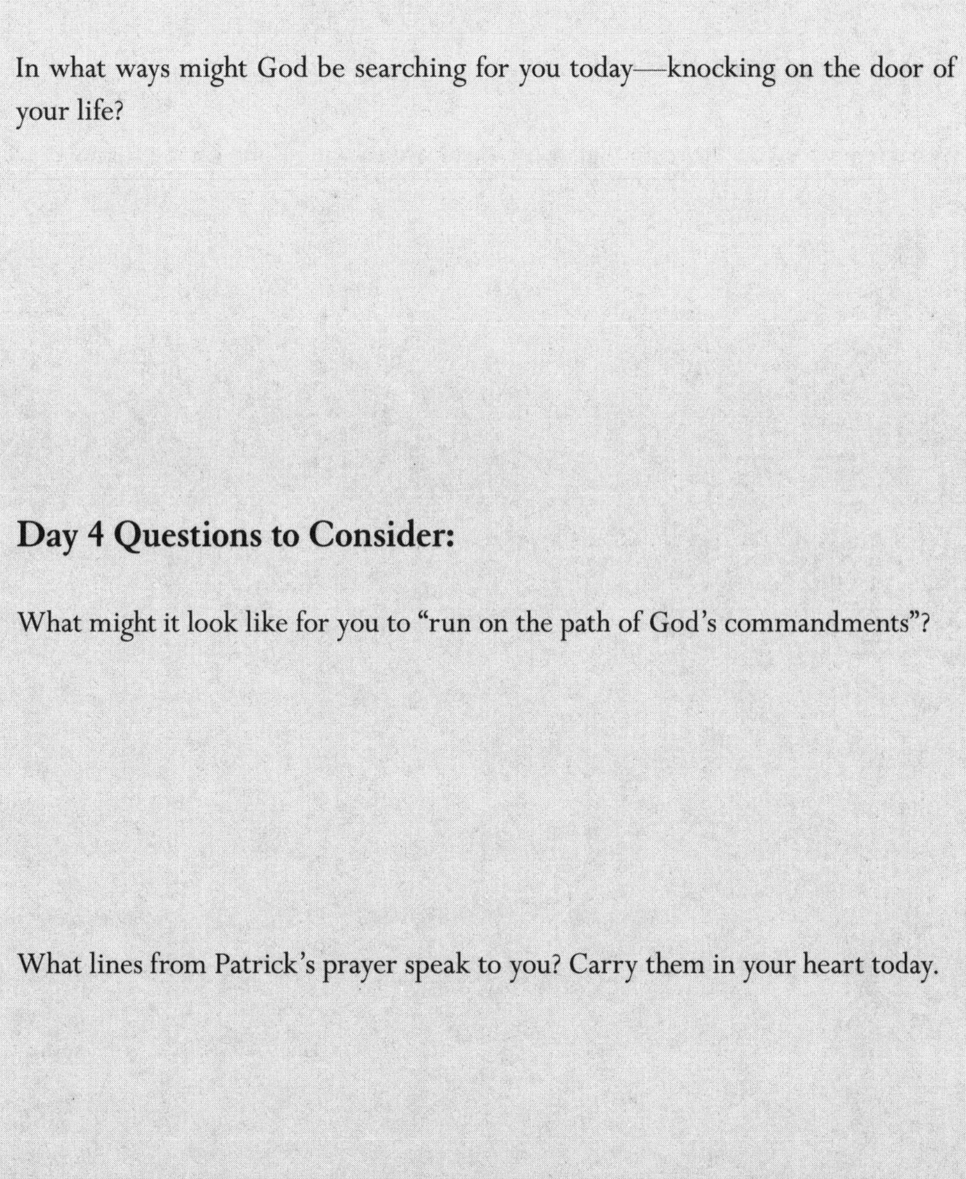

In what ways might God be searching for you today—knocking on the door of your life?

Day 4 Questions to Consider:

What might it look like for you to "run on the path of God's commandments"?

What lines from Patrick's prayer speak to you? Carry them in your heart today.

Day 5 Questions to Consider:

What fears are you carrying that you can release to your Abba Father today?

What might it look like for God's love to invade and fill you, guiding you to what you must do?

Leader's Guide

This *Emotionally Healthy Spirituality Course* (Part 1) provides an indispensable foundation to integrate a larger, deeper, beneath-the-surface discipleship paradigm into your church. But it is important to remember that this is only Part 1 of a two-part Course called Emotionally Healthy Discipleship.

Overview of the Course

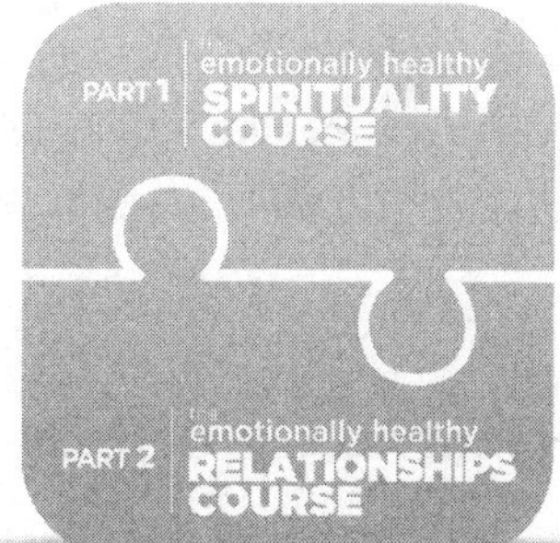

EH Spirituality (Part 1) has been designed and structured to offer a high-quality teaching experience with a trained Point Leader while at the same time offering close community support at a small group table.

Why?

At New Life Fellowship Church and churches around the world, we realized that this content was so critical that it needed to be offered in a centralized format that would ensure a high-quality experience for participants.

First, we wanted every newcomer and member to grasp our core elements of following Jesus in a way that deeply transforms us. And, secondly, we wanted to ensure the long-term integration of Emotionally Healthy Discipleship into every aspect of the church. The radical, introductory call of discipleship found in the *EH Spirituality*

(Part 1) serves as both an entry point and an essential bridge into the larger EHS vision. For this reason, *EH Spirituality* (Part 1) is offered at least one or two times a year in churches, along with the *EH Relationships (*Part 2).

EH Spirituality (Part 1) equips us in a discipleship paradigm that deeply changes **our relationship with God**. *EH Relationships* (Part 2) then deeply changes **our relationship with others**. The two Courses together form the foundation of a powerful discipleship strategy.

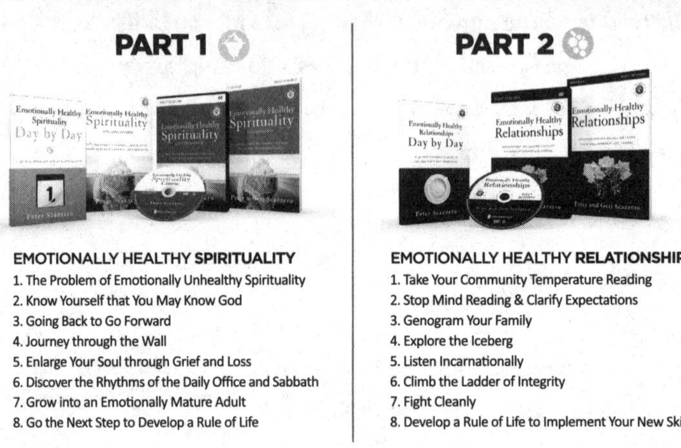

At New Life Fellowship Church our discipleship strategy builds on these two Courses. Go to www.emotionallyhealthy.org/vault to download a variety of excellent, free resources to help you serve as the Point Leader of the course or a small group table leader.

General Guidelines

1. Be sure to work through the workbook content before each session. Becoming familiar with the material and instructions will allow you to comfortably lead your group. You will also want to read the corresponding chapter(s) of the *Emotionally Healthy Spirituality* book before each session. If possible, we recommend you watch the video segments as well.

2. The Point Leader, or another appointed person, will need to select a Daily Office to open each session. The initial large-group Daily Office (for Session 1) is particularly challenging because it will be the first exposure to silence and stillness for many people. Have them turn to the appropriate page in the *EH Spirituality Day by Day* book and explain to them the elements of the Office before you begin. Refer to the Silence and Stillness guidelines below or display them on a PowerPoint slide as a brief orientation. While the Office may be difficult for some people, it will set a tone for the Course's centrality on being with Jesus. Specific suggestions on how to lead these Offices each week, and what you might say each week as an introduction, can be found at www.emotionallyhealthy.org/vault.

SILENCE & STILLNESS GUIDELINES

The Lord will fight for you; you need only to be still. Ex 14:14

- **Sit down and take a few deep breaths to settle into the silence.**
- **Choose a very simple prayer to express your openness and desire for God.**
  (e.g. Abba, Father, Holy Spirit, Jesus, Here I am Lord)
- **Close your eyes and offer this prayer to Jesus, allowing His will and love full access in your life.**
- **When you become distracted, offer again your simple prayer back to God.**

3. Each session is divided into six sections:
   - Introduction
   - Growing Connected
   - Video: Introduction
   - Group Discussion
   - Application
   - Video: Closing Summary

   The combination of doing a Daily Office together, watching the video presentations, and taking part in group and individual activities will require 90–120 minutes to complete. Respect everyone by beginning and ending on time.

4. Have extra copies of this workbook, the *Emotionally Healthy Spirituality* book, and the *Emotionally Healthy Day by Day* devotional available for each participant to purchase at the first two sessions. Make scholarships available, if possible, for those who need financial assistance.
5. This course (as well as *EH Relationships* [Part 2]) has been done successfully online with participants from all over the world. Tips for leading the Course online (e.g., via Zoom) can be found at www.emotionallyhealthy.org/vault. If you are doing the Course through Zoom, be sure the lighting and distances of people from their cameras are sufficient so people can see one another easily.
6. Set up the meeting room in a way that will comfortably seat all participants, preferably at a table so that everyone can see each other. Arrive at least 15 minutes ahead of time to greet group members individually as they come in.
7. The nature of this material easily lends itself to lengthy sharing. One of your greatest challenges as the small group table leader will be to keep the group focused and to share within the time frames allotted for each part of the session. Remember that each of these sessions could easily have been expanded into its own course. We have kept them together to serve a biblical framework that serves as an introduction into a life with God that goes beyond "tip of the iceberg spirituality." The implementation of these truths will involve the rest of people's lives.
8. If your table small group is large, you may want to break into smaller groups of three to four people so that everyone has a chance to participate.
9. When appropriate, it will be helpful if you lead by example—being vulnerable and open with life examples from your own journey. Remember, we are only experts on *our own* journey.
10. Respect where each person is in their journey with Christ. The Holy Spirit will prompt and lead each person differently and at different paces through this material. Remember that people change slowly—that includes you!
11. Being with Jesus is the core of both *EH Spirituality* (Part 1) and *EH Spirituality* (Part 2). Learning the practice of silence to listen and *be with God* two or three times a day is the core discipline leading to a deep personal transformation. You will want to be sure to faithfully meet with God each day in the silence

and stillness using *Emotionally Healthy Spirituality Day by Day: A 40 Day Journey with the Daily Office* and encourage participants to do the same.

Beginning in Session 2, in the "Growing Connected" section, we ask a question each week to emphasize the importance of people connecting firsthand with Jesus during the week through the *EH Spirituality Day by Day* devotional (and especially around silence and stillness).

Additional Suggestions[1]

1. Avoid answering your own questions. Feel free to rephrase a question.
2. Encourage more than one answer to each question. Ask, "What do the rest of you think?" or "Anyone else?"
3. Try to be affirming whenever possible. Let people know you appreciate their contributions.
4. Try not to reject an answer. If it is clearly wrong, ask, "What in the passage led you to that conclusion?"
5. Avoid going off on tangents. If people wander off course, gently bring them back to the subject at hand.

Specific Guidelines for Each Session

SESSION 1: The Problem of Emotionally Unhealthy Spirituality

In addition to the general guidelines, here are a few other key items for each session that you may find helpful.

Before the Session

- Read chapter 1 of the book *Emotionally Healthy Spirituality.*
- Select a Daily Office from Week 1 of *Emotionally Healthy Spirituality Day by Day* to begin the session. You will need 2–3 minutes to introduce the ideas of the Daily Office and stillness/silence. See point 2 under General Guidelines, page 105.

Introduction

- Be sure to read aloud the "Guidelines for the Group" (pages xi–xii) at the first two sessions.

Growing Connected

- This first "Growing Connected" section is longer than most to allow time for the Guidelines to be reviewed and for people to get to know one another with the second question: "Share your name and a few words about what makes you feel fully alive." You will want to think about this beforehand so you can give a concrete example from your own life.

Bible Study

- (*Question 1*) The fact that Saul was instructed by God to "attack the Amalekites and totally destroy all that belongs to him" (1 Samuel 15:3) raises the difficult question of why God would tell him to do such a thing. It presents a large, difficult problem that theologians have wrestled with for 2,000 years. The Bible does not offer any clear-cut, definitive answer; it is surely one of the things we don't fully understand about God and his ways. Thus, we want to be careful not to give simplistic answers to the problem. Rather, we want to help people grapple with it in light of God's larger plan to enter our world to save us and make space for life to flourish.

  If this larger question comes up in your group, saying, "I don't know" is a great response—especially in light of the time constraints of session one.

  Yet a number of excellent books written on the topic may be of help to you and/or participants in the Course who are grappling with this: Christopher Wright, *The God I Don't Understand: Reflections on Tough Questions of Faith* (Grand Rapids: Zondervan, 2008); L. Daniel Hawk, *The Violence of Biblical God: Canonical Narrative and Christian Faith* (Grand Rapids: Eerdmans, 2019); and Eric A. Seibert, *The Violence of Scripture: Overcoming the Old Testament's Troubling Legacy* (Minneapolis: Fortress Press, 2012).
- (*Questions 1 and 2*) You will notice that the timing for the first two questions is short (allowing time for just 1–3 people to answer), but much longer time is given for the final questions where you will want as many people as possible

to respond. Why? These are the weightiest of the questions and where we want to apply Scripture to people's personal lives. You will notice this kind of progression in all the Bible studies.

- (*Question 2*) Some possibilities are:
    - He is unaware of his mixed motives.
    - He has an inflated sense of who he is rather than humility and a recognition of his absolute dependence on God.
    - He is not teachable.
    - He does not recognize he is pretending to be someone he is not (i.e., his false self).
- (*Question 3*) The following are examples of people doing religious activity, yet it remains disconnected from their life:
    - I believe God is love and I go to church, but I can't stand people at work who irritate, ignore, or hurt me.
    - I read the Bible a lot but am often agitated and impatient with others.
    - I serve in the church but spend little time developing my relationship with Jesus on my own.
    - I sing songs about Jesus' love but am judgmental to people who see the world differently than I do.
    - I say I'm a follower of Jesus, but I rarely pray and listen to him before making decisions.
- (*Question 4*) At times our false self has become such a part of who we are that we don't even realize it. The consequences—fear, self-protection, possessiveness, manipulation, self-destructive tendencies, self-promotion, self-indulgence, and a need to distinguish ourselves from others—are harder to hide. (*Emotionally Healthy Spirituality*, page 56)
- (*Question 4*) For those who have not read the book, you will want to explain the iceberg illustration found on page 17 of chapter 1 of *Emotionally Healthy Spirituality*.

SESSION 2: Know Yourself That You May Know God

In addition to the general guidelines, here are some other helpful items to note by section:

Before the Session

- Read chapter 2 of the book *Emotionally Healthy Spirituality*.
- Select a Daily Office from Week 2 of *Emotionally Healthy Spirituality Day by Day* to begin the session. Again, take extra time as needed to explain the Daily Office and stillness/silence. See point 2 under General Guidelines.

Introduction

- Again, read aloud the "Guidelines for the Group" (pages xi–xii).

Growing Connected

- Have copies of the *Emotionally Healthy Spirituality Course Workbook*, the *Emotionally Healthy Spirituality* book, and *Emotionally Healthy Spirituality Day by Day* devotional available for newcomers.
- (*Question 1*) This is the first time you'll debrief on the readings from *EH Spirituality Day by Day* that the group did the past week. Allow two or three people to share. We recommend about 7 minutes for debriefing and 10 minutes for question 2.
- (*Question 2*) Keep in mind that this question about people's dream job often offers to the speaker, as well as the group, a glimpse of their "true self" in surprising ways.

Starters

- You may want to reread the section "Discovering God's Will and Your Emotions" in *Emotionally Healthy Spirituality* (pages 48–49) for a brief summary of the role of feelings in discerning God's will.
- (*Questions 1 and 2*) This exercise may bring up significant pain in some of the members of the group (*ex.*: unresolved anger, sadness that has not been grieved, shame that has been masked). Remember that this is a limited exercise with one goal—to help people *begin* to be aware of how much is going on inside of them. This is not the time to fix or give advice. Giving people space to express their feelings is a gift enough. If "Pandora's box" opens for a member of the group, thank the person for their awareness and vulnerability and let them know that you would be glad to talk with them after the meeting, if they would like. It is important to recognize your role as facilitator/small group leader and not a

professional counselor. In some cases, you may want to direct them to get the help they need beyond the limits of your group.

Bible Study

- Again, you will notice that more time is given for the final two questions than the first two more observation-oriented questions.
- One very helpful way to clarify this process of growing into our true selves in a new way is through use of a new term: *differentiation*. It refers to a person's capacity to "define his or her own life's goals and values apart from the pressures of those around them." The key emphasis of differentiation is the ability to think clearly and carefully as another means, besides our feelings, of knowing ourselves.

  It involves the ability to separate who you are from who you are not. The degree to which you are able to affirm your distinct values and goals apart from the pressures around you (separateness), while remaining close to people important to you (togetherness), helps determine your level of differentiation. People who are highly differentiated—such as David in this Bible account—can choose how they want to behave without being controlled by the approval or disapproval of others. Intensity of feelings, high stress, or the anxiety of others around them does not overwhelm their capacity to think intelligently.

  If you have additional time in your group, you can add the following question: David's ability to have a solid sense of who he was and who he wasn't in the midst of great trials and pressure is, in modern terminology, called *differentiation*. If David had been less differentiated, how might he have responded to his brothers, to Saul, and to Goliath?
- (*Question 3*) Possible answers include:
  - He has a personal, living, vital relationship with God. (It is a lived experience, not simply head knowledge or religious activity.)
  - He is deeply in tune with himself.
  - He remembers the lion and the bear victories from his past (smaller but significant enough to give him courage to trust God here).
  - He has a good inner grasp of who he is (gift and talents)—"I'm a shepherd, good with a sling shot and stones. I'm not a professional soldier." Thus he takes off Saul's armor.

- He is able to speak clearly, honestly and respectfully on his own behalf —even to authority figures and those older than him.
- He does not need the approval of others (i.e., have a reflected self) for his "lovability" or "okayness."
- He is not easily angered by his family, Saul, or Goliath.
- He is not anxious.

SESSION 3: Going Back in Order to Go Forward

In addition to the general guidelines, here are some other helpful items to note by section:

Before the Session

- Read chapter 3 of the book *Emotionally Healthy Spirituality.*
- Select a Daily Office from Week 3 of *Emotionally Healthy Spirituality Day by Day* to begin the session.

Bible Study

- (*Question 3*) There is no way we can know for sure why Joseph weeps, but numerous possibilities exist. Perhaps he weeps because he knows that Jacob never left instructions that he should not harm the brothers. Maybe he realizes that they will never really change; they are still lying. Or it could be that they are finally admitting their terrible cruelty and sins against Joseph, and Joseph is weeping because his pain is finally validated or acknowledged. It could be that these are tears of joy as he realizes this is the fulfillment of his dream from Genesis 37, or that all the pain of his life has led to the truth of this moment when he must make a momentous decision of whether or not to forgive.

Application

- (*Question 1*) Encourage those who may have done work on their family of origin in some other setting, or even filled out the chart prior to the group meeting, to prayerfully ponder this exercise again. God often surprises us with fresh insights when we have space to contemplate these messages before him.

SESSION 4: Journey through the Wall

In addition to the general guidelines, here are some other helpful items to note by section:

Before the Session

- Read chapter 4 of the book *Emotionally Healthy Spirituality.*
- Select a Daily Office from Week 4 of *Emotionally Healthy Spirituality Day by Day* to begin the session.

Growing Connected

- (*Question 2*) Last week, in "Going Back in Order to Go Forward," we talked about the messages we received from our families of origin. This week we focus on wrong messages we've received about God, such as: "Bad things won't happen to me if I obey God." "If you delight in the Lord, he will grant you everything you want." "Following Jesus will result in a prosperous, healthy, and great life—without too many problems." "If you accept Jesus, you'll live happily ever after."

Starters

- It usually takes a while (sometimes a long while!) to share about a Wall in a person's life. In light of only having a limited time for this question, you may want to use the time to share about a Wall that *you* have experienced, modeling how to do this in a limited time frame. We have found, at times, a well-thought-out testimony can sometimes be better than open sharing at this point. That may mean, however, that only two or three people will have time to share.

Bible Study

- (*Question 4*) We often carry within us inaccurate beliefs, or ideas, about God. For example, we take "Take delight in the Lord and he will give you the desires of your heart" (Psalm 37:4) to mean that if we are doing all we think God wants, then only good things will follow. The problem is that this contradicts other Scriptures such as our text here. Abraham was, as far as Scripture indicates, doing God's will. Yet it surely was not the desire of Abraham's heart to kill his son! Job is another classic example. He is an innocent sufferer—what makes his life so bewildering is the undeserved nature of his pain. The principle that we reap what we sow (Galatians 6:7–8) did not apply to Job, as his friends argued in Job chapters 3–37. For this reason, embracing our Walls frequently results in a crisis of faith for many believers rather than a doorway to transformation.

SESSION 5: Enlarge Your Soul through Grief and Loss

In addition to the general guidelines, here are some other helpful items to note by section:

Before the Session

- Read chapter 5 of the book *Emotionally Healthy Spirituality.*
- Select a Daily Office from Week 5 of *Emotionally Healthy Spirituality Day by Day* to begin the session.

Bible Study

- *(Question 1)* This list is explained in the chapter on grief and loss in the *Emotionally Healthy Spirituality* book, so you can refer people to those pages if you like.
- *(Question 2)* Jesus felt deeply his sorrow and pain. He did not "spin" or spiritualize it away. Jesus openly admitted his grief to those close to him and asked for their support. He repeatedly prayed to his Father for an alternative, but finally accepted the Father's "no." We see him move through a process from struggling to accept the Father's will to finally rising up to embrace it.

Application

- *(Question 2)* If you have the time, you could do a "Go Round" to give a chance for everyone to share what it was like for them to fill out the chart (e.g., "I don't do sadness, so it was really hard"; "It felt like opening Pandora's box"; "I needed a week.")
- *(Question 3)* Again, if you have time, you may want to expand this question, asking:
    - What pain are you not **Paying Attention** to?
    - What are you not bringing to God or **Waiting on God** with?
    - Are you allowing **Something New** to come out of the loss/pain?

As you take your participants through the application questions, keep in mind that we are ultimately wanting to help them see or respond to: *"What might be God's invitation for you?"*

- (*Question 3*) Two questions frequently come up in relation to grieving.
  1. How do I know I am grieving or if I should be grieving?

     One way to know if you are grieving is when you experience some of the following symptoms that normally accompany the stages of grieving—depression, anger, disbelief, yearning, bargaining. On the other hand, if you go through a significant loss but do not experience any of the above feelings, you may need a mature, objective outsider to help you move through the process.
  2. How do I know when I am done grieving?

     There are many factors that impact the amount of time needed to grieve. For example, the deeper the loss, the more time needed to grieve. The loss felt when a child leaves home and goes off to college is very different from the loss experienced should that child die tragically. Another factor is to respect how God has crafted each of us differently. The time you need and I need may be very different. One key principle is to not censor your emotions that come bubbling up as a result of the loss. Allow yourself, like Jesus and David, to feel them deeply before God. Censoring certain feelings because they are "bad" will only prolong or abort the discipleship process needed for long-term transformation in our lives.

SESSION 6: Discover the Rhythms of the Daily Office and Sabbath

In addition to the general guidelines, here are some other helpful items to note by section:

Before the Session

- Read chapter 6 of the book *Emotionally Healthy Spirituality*. The key word in this session is the word *rhythms*—in our days and weeks. Since we have been modeling Daily Offices each week, and talking about people's progress each week in developing a daily rhythm, the focus of this study will be on Sabbath.
- Select a Daily Office from Week 6 of *Emotionally Healthy Spirituality Day by Day* to begin the session.

Starters

- The Daily Office is a learned practice that takes time. For some it will be difficult; for others it will not be long enough. Others will struggle with all their interior noise. Be ready for a wide variety of responses. Hopefully, many will have adjusted comfortably to the rhythm of the Daily Office if they have been doing it since the Course began. For additional free resources on the Daily Office, go to www.emotionallyhealthy.org/vault.

Bible Study

- (*Question 2*) The concept of the Daily Office has a rich history going back to David, Daniel, the Jews during Jesus' time, and the early church. It is the rhythm of stopping to be with God at set times so that we can "practice the presence of God" all through our day when we are active. Daniel seamlessly models this for us. Jesus, of course, does this for us as well as we observe him getting alone to pray often (Luke 4:42–44; 5:12; 6:12–13; 11:1).
- (*Question 4*) An alternative question might be: "What are the obstacles for you to establish a consistent 24-hour period each week for Sabbath?"

Application

- The specific questions people have may go beyond the FAQs listed on pages 68–71. It is okay to say, "I don't know" and be comfortable in your own process of practicing Sabbath. For a larger treatment of the subject of Sabbath, read chapter 4, "Practice Sabbath Delight," in *The Emotionally Healthy Leader* (Zondervan, 2015). Another great resource is Wayne Mueller's *Sabbath: Finding Rest, Renewal, and Delight in Our Busy Lives* (New York: Bantam, 1999). Free sermons on Sabbath can also be found at www.emotionallyhealthy.org/media/sermons/. Finally, remember that the goal of this session is to provide people with an introduction to Sabbath, not to provide an exhaustive study.
- (*Question 3*) Depending on the size of your table group, and time available, you may want to keep your people together.

SESSION 7: Grow into an Emotionally Mature Adult

In addition to the general guidelines, here are some other helpful items to note by section:

Before the Session

- Read chapter 7 of the book *Emotionally Healthy Spirituality.*
- Select a Daily Office from Week 7 of *Emotionally Healthy Spirituality Day by Day* to begin the session.

Growing Connected

- (*Question 2*) You will want to go to pages 168–170 in chapter 7 that describes characteristics of emotional infants, children, adolescents, and adults.

Starters

- Be aware this can lead to a lively discussion! The following are examples of possible answers: we often emphasize spiritual productivity and gifts, often overlooking troublesome character traits; we also equate the knowledge of Scripture to spiritual maturity and ignore emotional immaturity; loving well is much more difficult to measure than content and doing ministry for God. So be prepared to end this discussion in the time allotted and move on to the next section.

Bible Study

- (*Question 5*) It is important that we maintain the creative tension and healthy balance between self-care and self-giving. Living at either extreme leads us to eventually resent people or ignore those in need around us altogether. The Samaritan stopped to help the hurting man. At the same time, he had the self-awareness and self-respect to recognize his own limits and decided to resume his own journey the next day. A healthy balance of self-care and self-giving in our lives is necessary in order to live out an "I-Thou" relationship both toward ourselves and others.

Application

- (*Questions 1 and 2*) Advise participants beforehand to avoid examples of expectations around moral issues or responsibilities (*ex.*: domestic abuse, adultery, parent's role in nurturing children, financial integrity in the church). These issues go beyond the scope of this exercise.

- (*Question 3*) You will want to review the Clarify Expectations Skill from the *EH Relationships Course*, Session 2 in preparation for this section.

  After discussing the answer to the question, you may also want to consider roleplaying with people in your group, helping them see what "healthy, mature" loving might look like.

  For example, you can play the person with whom they are clarifying the expectation, or you play them and roleplay clarifying an expectation with someone. We sometimes "play" them with them "playing," or being the person with whom they have an expectation. For example:

  Geri (playing Julie): *Candace, can I check out an expectation I realize I had of you but that you never agreed to?*

  Candace: *Sure.*

  Geri (playing Julie): *I had thought you would text me if you were going to be more than 15 minutes late for our meetings (I had never mentioned that, of course!) So, I'd like to now ask if you would be willing to do that, i.e., text me when you're running more than 15 minutes late?*

  Candace: *Sure, Julie, I can do that.*

SESSION 8: Go the Next Step to Develop a "Rule of Life"

In addition to the general guidelines, here are some other helpful items to note by section:

Before the Session

- Read chapter 8 of the book *Emotionally Healthy Spirituality.*
- Select a Daily Office from Week 8 of *Emotionally Healthy Spirituality Day by Day* to begin the session.

Bible Study

- Please note that this Bible Study section is intentionally only 15 minutes. We have placed the weight of this final meeting on the "Application" section, which requires about 45 minutes.
- (*Question 2*) Notice that there is no hint of legalism or "shoulds" in the description of the church in Acts. Jesus said, "Come to me, all you who are weary. . . .

My yoke is easy and my burden is light" (Matthew 11:28–30). In the same way, any healthy Rule of Life we develop needs to fit how God made us at this particular season of our life.

Application

- The final Application time is the most important part of this session. And, in particular, the final Group Time (*Question 2*) is most critical, as it will provide people a summary of the entire Course and give groups a sense of healthy closure. Be sure to pace the session accordingly so this time doesn't get cut short.
- Additional Option: If you have time, or can extend the session by 15 minutes, invite people from different table groups to share with the entire class, completing the sentence stem: *As a result of this Course, I am beginning to realize.* This gives people an even larger sense of what God has been doing in your midst during these 8 weeks! Geri and I rarely teach this class without adding this to our ending of the Course.

Notes

Session 1: The Problem of Emotionally Unhealthy Spirituality

1. For a more complete understanding of what we mean by emotional health and contemplative spirituality, see the book *Emotionally Healthy Spirituality*, pages 212–213.
2. See *Emotionally Healthy Spirituality*, pages 212–213.

Session 7: Grow into an Emotionally Mature Adult

1. For a fuller discussion of Martin Buber's distinction between "I-It" and "I-Thou" relationships, see *Emotionally Healthy Spirituality*, 172–175.
2. This exercise is adapted from Pat Ennis, *The Third Option: An Ongoing Program to Build Better Marriages*, Teachers Manual, Topic #3, "Expectations," 1–9.

Session 8: Go the Next Step to Develop a "Rule of Life"

1. Remember, a Rule of Life is simply an intentional, conscious plan to keep God at the center of everything we do. It provides guidelines to help us continually remember God as the source of our lives. It includes our unique combination of spiritual practices that provide structure and direction for us to intentionally pay attention and remember God in everything we do.

Leader's Guide

1. Adapted from James F. Nyquist and Jack Kuhatschek, *Leading Bible Discussions* (Downers Grove, Ill.: InterVarsity Press, 1985).

About the Authors

Geri Scazzero is the author of the bestselling *The Emotionally Healthy Woman*, *The Emotionally Healthy Woman Workbook*, and coauthor of *The Emotionally Healthy Relationships Course*. She is also, along with her husband Pete, the cofounder of Emotionally Healthy Spirituality, equipping the church in a discipleship that deeply changes lives.

Geri has served on staff at New Life Fellowship Church in New York City for the last twenty-nine years and is a popular speaker to pastors, church leaders, and at women's conferences—both in North America and internationally.

Connect with Geri on Facebook **(www.facebook.com/GeriScazzero)**.

Pete Scazzero, along with his wife, Geri, are the founders of Emotionally Healthy Discipleship, a ground-breaking ministry that moves the church forward by slowing the church down, in order to multiply deeply changed leaders and disciples. This journey began when Pete founded New Life Fellowship Church in Queens, New York, a large, multiracial church with more than seventy-three countries represented—where he served as the senior pastor for twenty-six years.

Pete hosts the top ranked Emotionally Healthy Leader podcast and is the author of a number of bestselling books, including *Emotionally Healthy Discipleship*, *The Emotionally Healthy Leader* and *Emotionally Healthy Spirituality*. He is also the author of the *Emotionally Healthy Discipleship Course* (Part 1 and 2) that has transformed tens of thousands of lives around the world. For more information, visit emotionallyhealthy.org or connect with Pete on Twitter, Facebook, or Instagram @petescazzero.

For more information, visit emotionallyhealthy.org.

EMOTIONALLY HEALTHY **SPIRITUALITY** COURSE

SESSION #	EHS BOOK	DAY-BY-DAY	WORKBOOK	VIDEO (or live)
1. The Problem of Emotionally Unhealthy Spirituality	☐ Read Chapter 1	☐ Prayerfully read Intro & Week 1	☐ Read Intro and fill out Session 1	☐ Watch Session 1
2. Know Yourself That You May Know God	☐ Read Chapter 2	☐ Prayerfully read Week 2	☐ Fill out Session 2	☐ Watch Session 2
3. Going Back in Order to Go Forward	☐ Read Chapter 3	☐ Prayerfully read Week 3	☐ Fill out Session 3	☐ Watch Session 3
4. Journey through the Wall	☐ Read Chapter 4	☐ Prayerfully read Week 4	☐ Fill out Session 4	☐ Watch Session 4
5. Enlarge Your Soul through Grief and Loss	☐ Read Chapter 5	☐ Prayerfully read Week 5	☐ Fill out Session 5	☐ Watch Session 5
6. Discover the Rhythms of the Daily Office and Sabbath	☐ Read Chapter 6	☐ Prayerfully read Week 6	☐ Fill out Session 6	☐ Watch Session 6
7. Grow into an Emotionally Healthy Adult	☐ Read Chapter 7	☐ Prayerfully read Week 7	☐ Fill out Session 7	☐ Watch Session 7
8. Go the Next Step to Develop a "Rule of Life"	☐ Read Chapter 8	☐ Prayerfully read Week 8	☐ Fill out Session 8	☐ Watch Session 8

Congratulations on completing **The Emotionally Healthy (EH) Spirituality Course**, the first half of The EH Discipleship Courses.

Go to ***emotionallyhealthy.org*** to receive your **Certificate of Completion.**